INTERNATIONAL MONETAF

CW00957494

GLOBAL FINANCIAL STABILITY REPORT

Navigating the High-Inflation Environment

2022
OCT

©2022 International Monetary Fund

IMF CSF Creative Solutions Division
Composition: AGS, An RR Donnelley Company

Cataloging-in-Publication Data

IMF Library

Names: International Monetary Fund.
Title: Global financial stability report.
Other titles: GFSR | World economic and financial surveys, 0258-7440
Description: Washington, DC : International Monetary Fund, 2002- | Semiannual | Some issues also have thematic
  titles. | Began with issue for March 2002.
Subjects: LCSH: Capital market—Statistics—Periodicals. | International finance—Forecasting—Periodicals. |
  Economic stabilization—Periodicals.
Classification: LCC HG4523.G557

ISBN 979-8-40021-967-2 (Paper)
     979-8-40022-153-8 (ePub)
     979-8-40022-151-4 (PDF)

Disclaimer: The *Global Financial Stability Report* (GFSR) is a survey by the IMF staff published twice a year, in the spring and fall. The report draws out the financial ramifications of economic issues highlighted in the IMF's *World Economic Outlook* (WEO). The report was prepared by IMF staff and has benefited from comments and suggestions from Executive Directors following their discussion of the report on September 29, 2022. The views expressed in this publication are those of the IMF staff and do not necessarily represent the views of the IMF's Executive Directors or their national authorities.

Recommended citation: International Monetary Fund. 2022. *Global Financial Stability Report—Navigating the High-Inflation Environment.* Washington, DC, October.

Please send orders to:
International Monetary Fund, Publications Services
P.O. Box 92780, Washington, DC 20090, U.S.A.
Tel.: (202) 623-7430 Fax: (202) 623-7201
E-mail: publications@imf.org
www.bookstore.imf.org
www.elibrary.imf.org

CONTENTS

Online Annexes

The following conventions are used throughout the *Global Financial Stability Report* (GFSR):

. . . to indicate that data are not available or not applicable;

— to indicate that the figure is zero or less than half the final digit shown or that the item does not exist;

– between years or months (for example, 2021–22 or January–June) to indicate the years or months covered, including the beginning and ending years or months;

/ between years or months (for example, 2021/22) to indicate a fiscal or financial year.

"Billion" means a thousand million.

"Trillion" means a thousand billion.

"Basis points" refers to hundredths of 1 percentage point (for example, 25 basis points are equivalent to ¼ of 1 percentage point).

If no source is listed on tables and figures, data are based on IMF staff estimates or calculations.

Minor discrepancies between sums of constituent figures and totals shown reflect rounding.

As used in this report, the terms "country" and "economy" do not in all cases refer to a territorial entity that is a state as understood by international law and practice. As used here, the term also covers some territorial entities that are not states but for which statistical data are maintained on a separate and independent basis.

The boundaries, colors, denominations, and any other information shown on the maps do not imply, on the part of the International Monetary Fund, any judgment on the legal status of any territory or any endorsement or acceptance of such boundaries.

Corrections and Revisions

The data and analysis appearing in the *Global Financial Stability Report* are compiled by the IMF staff at the time of publication. Every effort is made to ensure their timeliness, accuracy, and completeness. When errors are discovered, corrections and revisions are incorporated into the digital editions available from the IMF website and on the IMF eLibrary (see below). All substantive changes are listed in the online table of contents.

Print and Digital Editions

Print

Print copies of this *Global Financial Stability Report* can be ordered from the IMF bookstore at imfbk.st/523389.

Digital

Multiple digital editions of the *Global Financial Stability Report*, including ePub, enhanced PDF, and HTML, are available on the IMF eLibrary at www.elibrary.imf.org/OCT22GFSR.

Download a free PDF of the report and data sets for each of the charts therein from the IMF website at www.imf.org/publications/gfsr or scan the QR code below to access the *Global Financial Stability Report* web page directly:

Copyright and Reuse

Information on the terms and conditions for reusing the contents of this publication are at www.imf.org/external/terms.htm.

PREFACE

The *Global Financial Stability Report* (GFSR) assesses key vulnerabilities the global financial system is exposed to. In normal times, the report seeks to play a role in preventing crises by highlighting policies that may mitigate systemic risks, thereby contributing to global financial stability and the sustained economic growth of the IMF's member countries.

The analysis in this report was coordinated by the Monetary and Capital Markets (MCM) Department under the general direction of Tobias Adrian, Director. The project was directed by Fabio Natalucci, Deputy Director; Ranjit Singh, Assistant Director; Nassira Abbas, Deputy Division Chief; Charles Cohen, Deputy Division Chief; Antonio Garcia Pascual, Deputy Division Chief; Mahvash Qureshi, Division Chief; Mario Catalán, Deputy Division Chief; and Ananthakrishnan Prasad, Unit Chief. It benefited from comments and suggestions from the senior staff in the MCM Department.

Individual contributors to the report were Sergei Antoshin, Yingyuan Chen, Fabio Cortes, Reinout De Bock, Andrea Deghi, Xiaodan Ding, Dimitris Drakopoulos, Torsten Ehlers (Chapter 2 co-lead), Zhi Ken Gan, Charlotte Gardes-Landolfini (Chapter 2 co-lead), Deepali Gautam, Marco Gross, Pierre Guérin, Sanjay Hazarika, Anna-Theresa Helmke, Frank Hespeler, Shoko Ikarashi, Tara Iyer, Phakawa Jeasakul, Esti Kemp, Johannes Kramer, Harrison Kraus, Peter Lindner, Sheheryar Malik, Junghwan Mok, Kleopatra Nikolaou, Natalia Novikova, Thomas Piontek, Silvia Ramirez, Patrick Schneider, Xinyi Su, Felix Suntheim (Chapter 3 lead), Jeffrey David Williams, Hong Xiao, Yanzhe Xiao, Dmitry Yakovlev, Akihiko Yokoyama, and Xingmi Zheng.

Suellen Kelly Basilio, Javier Chang, Monica Devi, Olga Tamara Maria Lefebvre, and Srujana Sammeta were responsible for word processing.

Gemma Rose Diaz from the Communications Department led the editorial team and managed the report's production with editorial assistance from Denise Bergeron, David Einhorn, Harold Medina (and team), Lucy Scott Morales, Nancy Morrison, Grauel Group, and TalentMEDIA Services.

This issue of the GFSR draws in part on a series of discussions with banks, securities firms, asset management companies, hedge funds, standard setters, financial consultants, pension funds, trade associations, central banks, national treasuries, and academic researchers.

This GFSR reflects information available as of September 28, 2022. The report benefited from comments and suggestions from staff in other IMF departments, as well as from Executive Directors following their discussions of the GFSR on September 29, 2022. However, the analysis and policy considerations are those of the contributing staff and should not be attributed to the IMF, its Executive Directors, or their national authorities.

The global environment is fragile with storm clouds on the horizon. Inflation is now at multi-decade highs and broadly spread across countries. The economic outlook continues to deteriorate in many countries. At the same time, geopolitical risks persist. With these developments, the global financial stability outlook has deteriorated since the April 2022 *Global Financial Stability Report* (GFSR).

Confronting the specter of stubbornly high inflation, central banks in advanced economies and many emerging markets have had to move to an accelerated path of monetary policy normalization to prevent inflationary pressures from becoming entrenched. As an intended consequence of monetary tightening, global financial conditions have tightened in most regions.

Global financial markets have shown strains. Asset prices have sold off on the back of continued energy market pressures, emerging stress in cross-currency funding, and stress in certain nonbank financial institution segments. At the same time, market liquidity has deteriorated across key asset classes. There is a heightened risk of rapid, disorderly repricing which could interact with—and be amplified by—pre-existing vulnerabilities and poor market liquidity.

Rising uncertainty has additionally contributed to tighter financial conditions. Financial stability risks have increased, and the balance of risks is tilted to the downside. Financial vulnerabilities are elevated in the sovereign and nonbank financial institution sectors, where rising interest rates have brought on additional stress. A bright light comes from our global bank stress tests which show relative resilience for advanced economy banks.

The challenging macroeconomic and policy environment is also putting pressure on the global corporate sector. Large firms have reported a contraction in profit margins due to higher costs. Among small firms, bankruptcies have started to increase because of higher borrowing costs and declining fiscal support.

Many advanced economies and emerging markets may face housing-market-related risks as mortgage rates rise and lending standards tighten, squeezing potential borrowers out of the market.

Emerging markets are confronted with a multitude of risks from the strength of the US dollar, high external borrowing costs, stubbornly high inflation, volatile commodity markets, heightened uncertainty about the global economic outlook, and pressures from policy tightening in advanced economies. However, investors have continued to differentiate across emerging market economies, and many of the largest emerging markets seem to be more resilient to external vulnerabilities. Having said that, our updated global bank stress test shows that, in a severely adverse scenario, up to 29 percent of emerging market banks would breach capital requirements.

Pressures are particularly severe in frontier markets—generally smaller developing economies—where challenges are driven by a combination of tightening financial conditions, deteriorating fundamentals, and high exposure to commodity price volatility.

Navigating the uncharted waters of high inflation and tighter financial conditions requires a delicate balance by policymakers. Central banks must act resolutely to bring inflation back to target and avoid a de-anchoring of inflation expectations. Clear communication about their policy decisions, their commitment to their price-stability objectives, and the need to further normalize policy will be crucial to preserve credibility and avoid market volatility. At the same time, the tightening of financial conditions needs to be calibrated carefully, to aim at avoiding disorderly market conditions that could put financial stability unduly at risk.

The IMF's Integrated Policy Framework for emerging markets suggests a carefully calibrated mix of tools including interest rate policy, macroprudential actions, foreign exchange intervention, and capital flow measures. In the current environment, for many emerging markets, managing the global tightening cycle could involve a mix of tools to help mitigate stark monetary policy trade-offs and reduce financial stability risks.

Policymakers will also need to continue to scale up private climate finance, particularly in emerging market and developing economies. This includes efforts to require new financing instruments for climate-related investments in infrastructure, as well as the involvement of multilateral development banks to attract private investors, leveraging private investment and strengthening risk absorption capacity. The IMF will continue to help address climate change challenges through its financial stability risk assessments, lending through its new Resilience and Sustainability Trust, and advocating for improvements in the climate information architecture.

In addition, reform efforts for nonbank financial institutions have to continue. The role of open-ended funds featured prominently in the 2020 dash-for-cash episode, yet reforms have been lacking so far. Liquidity management tools, including swing pricing, should be considered seriously by policymakers.

Policymakers face an unusually challenging financial stability environment. If further adverse shocks were to realize, tighter financial conditions may trigger market illiquidity, disorderly sell-offs, or distress. Economic and financial market surveillance to act in a timely and well-informed manner and communicate clearly is crucial under such circumstances. I hope that this GFSR contributes to such timely and insightful surveillance.

Tobias Adrian
Financial Counsellor

The world economy is experiencing stubbornly high inflation, a challenge it has not faced for decades. Following the global financial crisis, with inflationary pressures muted, interest rates were extremely low for years and investors became accustomed to low volatility. The resulting easing of financial conditions supported economic growth, but it also contributed to a buildup of financial vulnerabilities. Now, with inflation at multidecade highs, monetary authorities in advanced economies are accelerating the pace of policy normalization. Policymakers in emerging markets have continued to tighten policy against a backdrop of rising inflation and currency pressures, albeit with notable differences across regions. Global financial conditions have tightened notably this year, leading to capital outflows from many emerging and frontier market economies with weaker macroeconomic fundamentals. Amid heightened economic and geopolitical uncertainties, investors have aggressively pulled back from risk-taking in September. With conditions worsening in recent weeks, key gauges of systemic risk, such as higher dollar funding costs and counterparty credit spreads, have risen. There is a risk of a disorderly tightening of financial conditions that may be amplified by vulnerabilities built over the years. The report will focus on the risks to global financial stability in the current macro-financial environment—an environment that is new to many policymakers and market participants.

The global economic outlook has deteriorated materially since the April 2022 *Global Financial Stability Report* (GFSR). A number of downside risks have crystallized, including higher-than-anticipated inflationary pressures, a worse-than-expected slowdown in China on the back of COVID-19 outbreaks and lockdowns, and additional spillovers from Russia's invasion of Ukraine. As a result, the slowdown of the global economy has intensified.

Amid extraordinary uncertainty about the outlook and stubbornly high inflation, central banks have continued to normalize policy to restore price stability. Global financial conditions have tightened in most regions since the April 2022 GFSR (Figure 1)—partly an intended consequence of tighter monetary policy and partly due to rising uncertainty about the outlook since April. By contrast, conditions in China have eased somewhat, as policymakers have provided additional support to offset a deterioration in the economic outlook and strains in the real estate sector.

Global financial stability risks have increased since the April 2022 GFSR, and the balance of risks is significantly skewed to the downside. The range of adverse GDP growth outcomes based

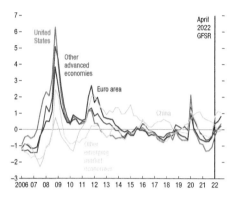

Figure 1. Global Financial Conditions in Selected Regions
(Standard deviations from the mean)

Source: IMF staff calculations.
Note: GFSR = *Global Financial Stability Report.*

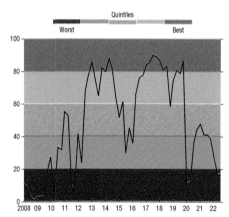

Figure 2. Near-Term Growth-at-Risk Forecast
(Percentile)

Sources: Bloomberg Finance L.P.; and IMF staff calculations.
Note: The black line traces the evolution of the 5th percentile threshold (the growth-at-risk metric) of near-term growth forecast densities.

Figure 3. Emerging Market Hard Currency Sovereign Spreads
(Basis points)

Sources: Bloomberg L.P.; and IMF staff calculations.
Note: HY = high yield; IG = investment grade.

Figure 4. Market-Implied Probability Distributions of Inflation Outcomes

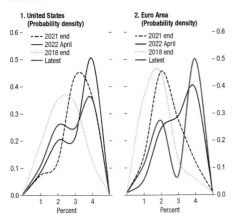

Sources: Bloomberg L.P.; and IMF staff calculations.

Figure 5. US Treasury Bid-Ask Spread and Market Liquidity Index
(Basis points)

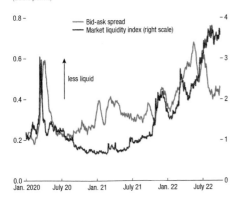

Sources: Bloomberg Finance L.P.; JPMorgan Chase & Co.; and IMF calculations.
Note: The market liquidity index is the average of Bloomberg US Government Securities Liquidity index and the JP Morgan US Treasury total root mean square error (RMSE) index.

Figure 6. Emerging Market Local Currency Bond and Equity Flows
(Cumulative, billions of US dollars)

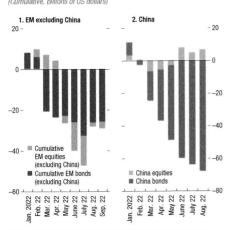

Sources: Bloomberg Finance L.P.; national sources; and IMF staff calculations.
Note: EM = emerging market.

on the probability distribution of future GDP growth is in the worst 20th percentile of the last four decades (Figure 2). Financial vulnerabilities are elevated in the sovereign and nonbank financial institution sectors, while market liquidity has deteriorated across some key asset classes.

Interest rates and prices of risk assets have been extremely volatile since April, reflecting heightened uncertainty about the economic and policy outlook. Risk assets sold off sharply through June on fears that central banks would have to step up the pace of policy rate hikes to fight high inflation. Emerging market assets suffered large losses, and sovereign spreads of high-yield emerging markets rose nearly to levels last seen in March 2020 (Figure 3). Crypto markets also experienced extreme volatility leading to the collapse of some of the riskiest segments and the unwinding of some crypto funds.

In the middle of the year, as recession fears grew, risk assets rallied on hopes that the monetary policy normalization cycle would end sooner than previously anticipated. These moves, however, have been unwound and risk assets have experienced further losses, as major central banks have strongly reaffirmed their resolve to fight inflation and meet their price stability mandates.

Disagreement among investors around the most likely inflation outcomes appears to have become more notable. In the euro area, there are significant odds of both low- and high-inflation outcomes, likely reflecting heightened concerns about a slowdown in aggregate growth (Figure 4). There is a risk, however, that a rapid, disorderly repricing of risk in coming months could interact with, and be amplified by, preexisting vulnerabilities and poor market liquidity.

Market liquidity metrics have worsened across asset classes, including in markets that are generally highly liquid and among standardized and exchange-traded products. US Treasury bid-ask spreads have widened significantly, market depth has declined sharply, and liquidity premiums have increased (Figure 5).

European financial markets have shown strains since the April 2022 GFSR. Asset prices have sold off on the back of growing recession fears amid natural gas shortages and the reemergence of fragmentation risks in the euro area. However, spreads of southern European government bond yield over German yields tightened after the European Central Bank's announcement of a new tool to fight fragmentation in the euro area, the Transmission Protection Instrument. In the UK, investor concerns about the fiscal and inflation outlook following the announcement of large debt-financed tax cuts and fiscal measures to deal with high energy prices weighed heavily on market sentiment. The British pound depreciated abruptly, and sovereign bond prices dropped sharply. To prevent dysfunction in the gilt market from posing a material risk to UK financial stability, the Bank of England, in line with its financial stability mandate, announced on September 28 temporary and targeted purchases of long-dated UK government bonds.

Central banks in emerging and frontier markets have also continued to tighten monetary policy. But regional differences remain stark, with some countries hiking policy rates earlier and more aggressively in response to inflationary pressures. Conditions in local currency bond markets have worsened materially, reflecting concerns about the macroeconomic outlook and rising debt levels. Sovereign bond term premiums have increased sharply, especially for central and eastern Europe.

Emerging markets face a multitude of risks stemming from high external borrowing costs, stubbornly high inflation, volatile commodity markets, heightened uncertainty about the global economic outlook, and pressures from policy tightening in advanced economies. Pressures are particularly acute in frontier markets, where challenges are driven by a combination of tightening financial conditions, deteriorating fundamentals, and high exposure to commodity price volatility. Interest expenses on government debt have continued to rise, increasing immediate liquidity pressures. In an environment of poor fundamentals and lack of investor risk appetite, defaults may follow. However, investors have continued to differentiate across emerging market economies so far, and many of the largest emerging markets seem to be more resilient to external vulnerabilities. Nonresident portfolio flows remain weak despite some signs of stabilization after sizable outflows in the first half of the year (Figure 6). Issuance of sovereign hard currency bonds has deteriorated sharply. Without an improvement in market access, many frontier market issuers will have to seek alternative funding sources and/or debt reprofiling and restructurings.

The challenging macroeconomic environment is also pressuring the global corporate sector. Credit spreads have widened substantially across sectors since April. Large firms have reported a contraction in profit margins due to higher costs, while downward revisions to global earnings growth forecasts appear to be gaining momentum on concerns about a possible recession. At small firms, bankruptcies have already started to increase in major advanced economies because these firms are more affected by rising borrowing costs and declining fiscal support. Companies that rely on leveraged finance markets are facing tighter lending terms and standards against a challenging growth backdrop. The credit quality of these assets may be tested during an economic downturn, with potential spillovers to the broader macroeconomy.

As central banks aggressively tighten monetary policy, soaring borrowing costs and tighter lending standards, coupled with stretched valuations after years of rising prices, could adversely affect housing markets. In a worst-case scenario, real house price declines could be significant, driven by affordability pressures and deteriorating economic prospects (Figure 7).

In China, the property sector downturn has deepened as a sharp decline in home sales during COVID-19 lockdowns has

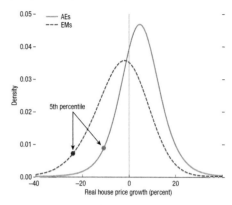

Figure 7. House Prices at Risk: Advanced Economies and Emerging Markets Three Years Ahead
(Density; cumulative growth in percent)

Sources: Bank for International Settlements; Bloomberg L.P.; Haver Analytics; IMF, World Economic Outlook database; and IMF staff calculations.
Note: AEs = advanced economies; EMs = emerging markets.

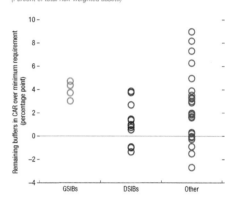

Figure 8. Potential Credit Losses for Chinese Banks Related to Real Estate Exposure
(Percent of total risk-weighted assets)

Sources: Bloomberg Finance L.P.; CEIC; S&P Capital IQ; and IMF staff calculations.
Note: CAR = capital adequacy ratio; DSIBs = domestic systemically important banks; GSIBs = global systemically important banks.

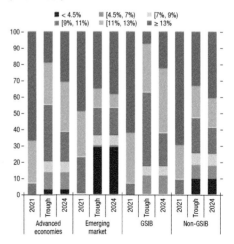

Figure 9. Distribution of Banks by Capital Adequacy in an Adverse Scenario
(Percent of assets)

Sources: Fitch Connect; and IMF staff calculations.
Note: The figure shows the composition of common equity Tier 1 (CET1). GSIB = global systemically important bank.

Figure 10. Sustainable Debt Issuance in EMDEs Grew Strongly in 2021, with a Notable Rise in Sustainability-Linked Instruments
(Billions of US dollars; percent)

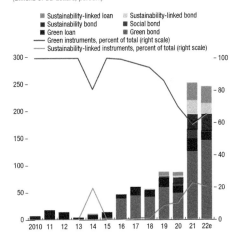

Sources: Bloomberg Finance L.P.; and IMF staff calculations.
Note: Share of green instruments and sustainability linked instruments is shown as a percent of total emerging market sustainable instrument issuance. 22e = annualized estimate for 2022; EMDEs = emerging market and developing economies.

Figure 11. Effect of Open-End Investment Fund Vulnerabilities on Bond Return Volatility
(Percent of median volatility)

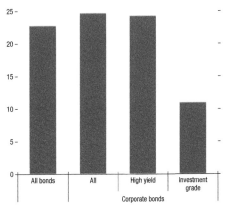

Sources: FactSet; Morningstar; Refinitiv Datastream; and IMF staff calculations.

exacerbated the liquidity stress of property developers, raising concerns about broader solvency risks. Property developer failures could spill over into the banking sector, affecting some vulnerable small banks and domestic systemically important banks, given their lower capital buffers and higher property-related concentration risk (Figure 8).

High levels of capital and ample liquidity buffers have bolstered the resilience of the global banking sector. However, the IMF's Global Bank Stress Test shows that, in a scenario with an abrupt and sharp tightening of financial conditions that would send the global economy into recession in 2023 amid high inflation, up to 29 percent of emerging market banks (by assets) would breach capital requirements, while most advanced economy banks would remain resilient. To rebuild buffers and the capital shortfall would require over $200 billion (Figure 9).

As outlined in Chapter 2, emerging market and developing economies will need significant climate financing in coming years to reduce their greenhouse gas emissions and to adapt to the physical effects of climate change. Sustainable finance has grown rapidly but emerging market and developing economies continue to be at a disadvantage. Decisively scaling up private climate finance faces significant challenges, including the lack of supportive climate policies (such as effective carbon pricing) and a still-weak climate information architecture (Figure 10).

Open-end investment funds are playing an increasingly important role in financial markets. However, the liquidity mismatch between their assets and liabilities raises financial stability concerns. Chapter 3 looks at how open-end funds holding illiquid assets while offering daily redemptions can be a key driver of fragility in asset prices by raising the likelihood of investor runs and asset fire sales (Figure 11). The vulnerabilities of open-end funds can also have cross-border spillover effects and lead to a tightening of overall domestic financial conditions, generating potential risks to macrofinancial stability.

Policy Recommendations

Central banks must act resolutely to bring inflation back to target, keeping inflationary pressures from becoming entrenched and avoiding de-anchoring of inflation expectations that would damage credibility. The high uncertainty clouding the outlook hampers the ability of policymakers to provide explicit and precise guidance about the future path of monetary policy. But clear communication about their policy reaction functions, their unwavering commitment to achieve their mandated objectives, and the need to further normalize policy is crucial to preserve credibility and avoid unwarranted market volatility.

According to the IMF's Integrated Policy Framework, where appropriate, some emerging market economies managing the global tightening cycle could consider using some combination of targeted foreign exchange interventions, capital flow measures, and/or other actions to help smooth exchange rate adjustments to reduce financial stability risks and maintain appropriate monetary policy transmission.

Sovereign borrowers in developing economies and frontier markets should enhance efforts to contain risks associated with their high debt vulnerabilities, including through early contact with their creditors, multilateral cooperation, and support from the international community. Enacting credible medium-term fiscal consolidation plans following the recent shocks could help contain borrowing and refinancing costs and alleviate debt sustainability concerns.

Policymakers should contain further buildup of financial vulnerabilities. While considering country-specific circumstances and the near-term economic challenges, they should adjust selected macroprudential tools as needed to tackle pockets of elevated vulnerabilities. Striking a balance between containing the buildup of vulnerabilities and avoiding procyclicality and a disorderly tightening of financial conditions is important given heightened economic uncertainty and the ongoing policy normalization process.

Implementation of policies to mitigate market liquidity risks is paramount to avoid possible amplification of shocks. Supervisory authorities should monitor the robustness of trading infrastructures and support transparency in markets. In addition, improving the availability of data at the trade level would help with

timely assessment of liquidity risks. Given the increasing importance of nonbank financial institutions, counterparties should carefully monitor intraday activity and leverage exposures, strengthen their liquidity risk management practices, and enhance transparency and data availability.

Scaling up private climate finance will require new finance instruments and the involvement of multilateral development banks to attract private investors, leveraging private investment and strengthening risk absorption capacity. A larger share of equity financing and additional resources for climate finance from multilateral development banks would help countries achieve these objectives. The IMF can help its members address climate change challenges by undertaking financial stability risk assessments, lending through its new Resilience and Sustainability Trust, and advocating for closing data gaps and disclosures.

Policy action is warranted to mitigate vulnerabilities and risks associated with open-end investment funds. Price-based liquidity management tools such as swing pricing can be effective in lowering asset price fragilities but policymakers should provide further guidance on their implementation. Additional tools could include linking the frequency of redemptions to the liquidity of funds' portfolios. Policymakers should also consider tighter monitoring of funds' liquidity risk management practices, additional disclosures by open-end funds to better assess vulnerabilities, and measures to bolster the provision of liquidity.

The following remarks were made by the Chair at the conclusion of the Executive Board's discussion of the Fiscal Monitor, Global Financial Stability Report, *and* World Economic Outlook *on September 29, 2022.*

Executive Directors broadly agreed with staff's assessment of the global economic outlook, risks, and policy priorities. They broadly concurred that high inflation and associated tightening financial conditions resulting from policy normalization; the effects of Russia's war in Ukraine, particularly on food and energy prices; and the lingering COVID-19 pandemic, with its related supply chain disruptions, have all contributed to a weakening in global economic prospects. Directors recognized that risks to the outlook are unusually high. They agreed that the most prominent risks—including policy divergence and cross-border tensions, further energy and food price shocks, an entrenchment of inflation dynamics and a de-anchoring of inflation expectations, and debt vulnerabilities in some emerging markets—tilt the distribution of likely growth outcomes to the downside. Moreover, Directors recognized that the current environment of high inflation, slowdown in growth, and heightened uncertainty about the economic and policy outlook poses particularly difficult tradeoffs and challenges for policymakers, making the likelihood of a policy mistake higher than usual.

Against this backdrop, Directors agreed that the appropriate policy responses differ across countries, reflecting their local circumstances, their inflation and growth outlooks, and differences in trade and financial exposures. For most economies, they considered that tighter monetary and fiscal policies are necessary to durably reduce inflation. At the same time, they emphasized that these policies should be accompanied by structural reforms that improve productivity, expand economic capacity, and ease supply-side constraints. Directors recognized that many emerging market and developing economies (EMDEs) face tougher policy choices, as higher food and fuel prices, the need to support the recovery and vulnerable populations, and rising costs of market financing from tighter global financial conditions and US dollar appreciation can pull in different directions, necessitating a difficult balancing act.

Directors stressed that monetary authorities should act decisively and continue to normalize policy to prevent inflationary pressures from becoming entrenched and avoid an unmooring of inflation expectations. They agreed that central banks in most advanced economies and EMDEs would need to continue tightening the monetary policy stance to bring inflation credibly back to target and to anchor inflation expectations. Directors stressed that maintaining central bank independence and policy credibility will be essential to secure price stability. They also emphasized the importance of continuing to assess the impact of the simultaneous monetary tightening by central banks and, in particular, its implications for EMDEs. Directors stressed that clear communication of both policy functions and the unwavering commitment to achieve price objectives is crucial to preserve credibility and avoid unwarranted market volatility. They considered that, should global financial conditions tighten in a disorderly manner, EMDEs could face capital outflows and should be ready to use all available tools, including foreign exchange interventions and capital flow management measures, guided when appropriate by the Integrated Policy Framework and in line with the Institutional View on the Liberalization and Management of Capital Flows and without substituting for exchange rate flexibility and warranted macroeconomic adjustments.

Directors concurred that fiscal policy is operating in a highly uncertain environment of elevated inflation, slowdown in growth, high debt, and tightening borrowing conditions. They stressed that, where inflation is elevated, a tighter fiscal stance would send a powerful signal that policymakers are aligned in their fight against inflation. Such a signal would, in turn, reduce the size of required interest rate increases to keep inflation expectations anchored and would help keep borrowing costs lower. Directors emphasized that fiscal support to address the surge in cost of living from high food and energy prices should primarily focus on targeted support to the most vulnerable segments, given the criticality of preserving price incentives to promote energy conservation. Some Directors considered that additional but temporary energy policies may be needed in countries that face exceptionally high and volatile energy prices owing to Russia's war in Ukraine.

Directors broadly agreed that fiscal policy has a role in protecting people against loss in real incomes in moments of large adverse shocks, but that requires healthy public finances. Building on the experience of the pandemic, they considered that governments should invest in social safety nets and develop policy strategies and tools that can be readily deployed under various scenarios. Directors concurred that a sound and credible medium-term fiscal framework, including spending prioritization and efforts to raise revenues, can help manage urgent needs from high food and energy prices, rebuild fiscal buffers to cope with future crises, and make progress in long-term development needs, such as investment in renewable energy and health care, which can also foster economic resilience.

Directors noted that, although no material systemic event has materialized so far, financial stability risks have risen along many dimensions, which highlights the importance of containing a further buildup of financial vulnerabilities. Being mindful of country-specific circumstances and near-term economic challenges, they agreed that selected macroprudential tools may need to be adjusted to tackle pockets of elevated vulnerabilities. Directors noted, however, that striking a balance between containing the buildup of vulnerabilities and avoiding procyclicality and a disorderly tightening of financial conditions is important given heightened economic uncertainty and the ongoing policy normalization process.

Directors reiterated their urgent call for global cooperation and dialogue, which are essential to defuse geopolitical tensions, avoid further economic and trade fragmentation, and respond to challenges in an interconnected world. They agreed on the criticality of multilateral actions to respond to existing and unfolding humanitarian crises, end Russia's war in Ukraine, safeguard global liquidity, manage debt distress, mitigate and adapt to climate change, and end the pandemic. Noting that many countries are contending with tighter financial conditions, high debt levels, and pressures to protect the most vulnerable from surging inflation, Directors called on the multilateral institutions to stand ready to provide emergency liquidity to safeguard essential spending and contain financing crises. They also called for greater debt transparency and better mechanisms to produce orderly debt restructurings—including a more effective Common Framework—in those cases where insolvency issues prevail. Acknowledging that recent energy and food price shocks may have undermined the green transition, Directors stressed that achieving energy security and addressing the climate agenda go hand-in-hand, including by addressing the significant climate financing needs of EMDEs and investing in renewable energy and energy efficiency. Even though the COVID-19 pandemic is starting to fade, Directors called for decisive actions to address the continued inequity in access to health care and vaccinations worldwide and reduce the threat of future pandemics.

FINANCIAL STABILITY IN THE NEW HIGH-INFLATION ENVIRONMENT

Chapter 1 at a Glance

- Global financial stability risks have increased since the April 2022 *Global Financial Stability Report* and the balance of risks is skewed to the downside. Amid the highest inflation in decades and extraordinary uncertainty about the outlook, markets have been extremely volatile. Despite some gains midyear, prices of risk assets such as equities and corporate bonds have declined sharply, on balance, with investors aggressively pulling back from risk taking in September. A deterioration in market liquidity appears to have amplified price moves.
- Financial conditions have continued to tighten globally since April. In many advanced economies, financial conditions are tight by historical standards. In some emerging markets they have reached levels last seen during the height of the COVID-19 crisis. In contrast, conditions have eased some in China, as policymakers have provided additional support.
- With conditions worsening in recent weeks, key gauges of systemic risk, such as dollar funding costs and counterparty credit spreads, have risen. There is a risk of a disorderly tightening in financial conditions that may interact with preexisting vulnerabilities. Investors may further reassess the outlook if inflationary pressures do not abate as quickly as currently anticipated or the economic slowdown intensifies.
- In emerging markets, rising rates, worsening fundamentals, and large outflows have pushed up borrowing costs notably. The impact has been especially severe for more vulnerable economies, with 20 countries either in default or trading at distressed levels. Unless market conditions improve, there is a risk of further sovereign defaults in frontier markets. Large emerging market issuers with stronger fundamentals, by contrast, have proved resilient thus far.
- In China, the property downturn has deepened as sharp declines in home sales during lockdowns have exacerbated pressures on developers, with heightened risk of spillovers to the banking, corporate, and local government sectors. In many other countries, the housing market is still showing signs of overheating and there is a risk of a sharp fall in house prices as mortgage rates rise, affordability falls, and lending standards tighten.
- Global stress tests for banks show that, under a severe downturn scenario, up to 29 percent of emerging market bank assets could breach minimum capital requirements; in advanced economies most banks would remain resilient. Corporate credit is also facing increased risk of default, with sub-investment-grade firms more exposed to a turn in the credit cycle and deteriorating investor risk appetite.
- Central banks must act resolutely to bring inflation back to target, to keep inflationary pressures from becoming entrenched, and to avoid de-anchoring of inflation expectations that would damage credibility. The high uncertainty clouding the outlook hampers policymakers' ability to provide explicit and precise guidance about the future path of monetary policy. But clear communication about their policy function, their unwavering commitment to achieve their mandated objectives, and the need to further normalize policy is crucial to avoid unwarranted market volatility.
- Ensuring effective transmission of monetary policy is crucial during policy normalization. The Transmission Protection Instrument announced by the European Central Bank is a welcome step to address euro area fragmentation risks.
- According to the IMF's Integrated Policy Framework, where appropriate, some emerging market economies managing the global tightening cycle could consider using some combination of targeted foreign exchange interventions, capital flow measures, and/or other actions to help smooth exchange rate adjustments to reduce financial stability risks and maintain appropriate monetary policy transmission.

- Policymakers should contain a further buildup of financial vulnerabilities. While considering country-specific circumstances and the near-term economic challenges, they should adjust selected macroprudential tools as needed to tackle pockets of elevated vulnerabilities. Striking a balance between containing the buildup of vulnerabilities and avoiding procyclicality and a disorderly tightening of financial conditions is essential.
- Implementation of policies to mitigate market liquidity risks is key to avoid possible amplification of shocks, especially during monetary policy normalization. Counterparties should strengthen their liquidity risk management practices.

Financial Conditions Tighten as Central Banks Act Aggressively to Tame Inflation amid Extraordinary Uncertainty

The world economy is experiencing stubbornly high inflation, a challenge it has not faced for decades, amid heightened economic and geopolitical uncertainties and disruptions in energy and commodity markets stemming from the COVID-19 pandemic and Russia's ongoing war in Ukraine. Following the global financial crisis, with inflationary pressures muted, central banks kept interest rates extremely low for years and investors became accustomed to a low-volatility environment. The ensuing easing of financial conditions supported economic growth, but it also contributed to risk taking and a buildup of financial vulnerabilities—a risk highlighted in previous *Global Financial Stability Reports* (GFSRs).

Now, with inflation at multidecade highs, monetary authorities in advanced economies are accelerating the pace of policy normalization to prevent inflationary pressures from becoming entrenched and inflation expectations from de-anchoring. Policymakers in emerging markets, which had started to hike interest rates earlier in 2021, have continued to tighten policy against a backdrop of rising inflation and currency pressures, albeit with significant regional differences. Global financial conditions have tightened notably this year, partly an intended consequence of policy normalization, leading to capital outflows from many emerging and frontier market economies with weaker macroeconomic fundamentals. With the global economy facing a number of challenges and policymakers continuing to normalize policy to tame high inflation, there is a risk of a disorderly tightening of global financial conditions that may be amplified by vulnerabilities built over the years. This chapter will focus on some of the most pertinent conjunctural and structural vulnerabilities in

advanced economies and emerging markets in the current macro-financial environment—an environment that is new to many policymakers and market participants.[1]

The global economic outlook has worsened materially since the April 2022 GFSR. A number of downside risks have crystallized, including higher-than-anticipated inflationary pressures; a worse-than-expected slowdown in China on the back of COVID-19 outbreaks, lockdowns, and a further deterioration in real estate; and additional spillovers from Russia's invasion of Ukraine. As a result, the slowdown of the global economy has intensified, while inflation has remained stubbornly high (see the October 2022 *World Economic Outlook* [WEO]).

Most monetary authorities around the world have continued to tighten policy to tame inflation and restore price stability. In advanced economies, central banks have accelerated the pace of normalization. In emerging markets, where policymakers had already started to hike interest rates in 2021, tightening has continued to keep pace with rising inflation and currency pressures that have been exacerbated by higher rates in the United States and elsewhere. The global monetary policy stance has become tighter, with the number of central banks hiking the policy rate increasing markedly, but some differences are noteworthy. The Federal Reserve policy tightening cycle is leading other central banks in advanced economies. In contrast, in Japan, yield curve control has continued. Among emerging markets, the People's Bank of China policy easing stands in sharp contrast to other countries. The US dollar strength may contribute to inflationary pressures in some countries and lead to further tightening of policy in some countries.

Global financial conditions have tightened further, on balance, since the April 2022 GFSR, partly as

---

[1]Unless otherwise stated, the data cutoff date is September 28, 2022.

Figure 1.1. Global Financial Conditions

Financial conditions in advanced economies and emerging market economies have tightened further on net.

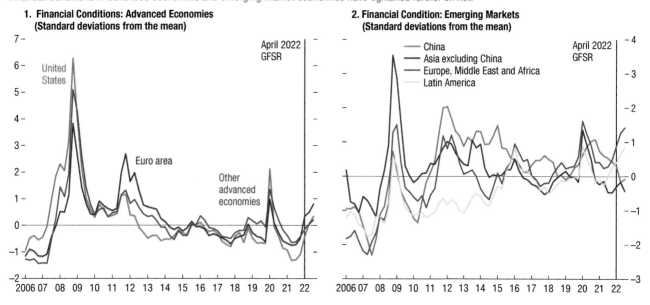

Sources: Bloomberg Finance L.P.; Haver Analytics; national data sources; and IMF staff calculations.
Note: The FCIs are calculated using the latest available variables. In the US, the Q2 and Q3 proxies use estimated real house prices based on the FHFA US house price index mom changes. In panel 2, the group "Europe, Middle East and Africa" excludes Russia, Türkiye and Ukraine. In Türkiye, local price signals have become less relevant recently due to idiosyncratic policy measures that incentivize holding lira assets. Panels 1 and 2 show quarterly averages for 2006–19 and monthly averages for 2020–22. Standard deviations are calculated over the period 1996–present. The IMF financial condition index is designed to capture the pricing of risk. It incorporates various pricing indicators, including real house prices. Balance sheet or credit growth metrics are not included. For details, please see the October 2018 GFSR annex. GFSR = *Global Financial Stability Report*.

an intended consequence of tighter monetary policy and partly due to rising uncertainty about the outlook (Figure 1.1, panel 1). In advanced economies, financial conditions have tightened rapidly and are now above historical averages in most countries, with higher interest rates and lower corporate valuations the key drivers behind the tightening.[2] Financial conditions are even tighter in some emerging markets. In central, eastern, and southern Europe, as well as in the Middle East and Africa, financial conditions are at levels last seen during the height of the COVID-19 crisis (Figure 1.1, panel 2). Weaker currencies and wider spreads on dollar funding have pushed up external borrowing costs. In contrast, conditions have eased somewhat in China, where policymakers have provided additional support to offset a rise in corporate credit borrowing costs stemming from strains among property developers and a deterioration in the economic outlook.

Interest rates and prices of risk assets (such as equities, corporate bonds, commodities, and currencies) have been very volatile since April, reflecting high levels of uncertainty about the inflation and growth outlook and implications for monetary policy. Risk assets sold off sharply through June on fears that central banks would have to step up the pace of interest rate hikes to fight high inflation and prevent inflation expectations from becoming unmoored. Markets pivoted for a while midyear as investors became increasingly concerned about rising recession risks. Boosted by hopes that the monetary cycle in advanced economies could end sooner than previously anticipated, risk assets experienced a relief rally, long-term interest rates fell, and financial conditions eased somewhat in July. In recent weeks, conditions in financial markets have deteriorated as major central banks have strongly reaffirmed their resolve to fight inflation and meet their price stability mandates.[3]

---

[2]Gains in house prices, albeit slowing since the beginning of the policy normalization process, have partly offset the tightening in financial conditions resulting from rising interest rates and sharply falling corporate valuations.

[3]See, for example, recent speeches delivered at the 2022 Jackson Hole policy symposium on "Monetary Policy and Price Stability," by Jerome Powell, chair of the Federal Reserve, and on "Monetary Policy and the Great Volatility," by Isabel Schnabel, member of the European Central Bank executive board.

Figure 1.2. Sell-Off in Risk Assets and Jump in Volatility

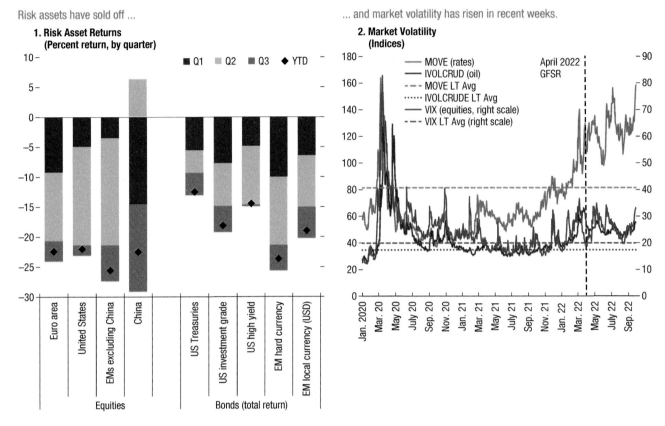

Risk assets have sold off ...

1. Risk Asset Returns
(Percent return, by quarter)

... and market volatility has risen in recent weeks.

2. Market Volatility
(Indices)

Sources: Bloomberg Finance L.P.; MSCI; and IMF staff calculations.
Note: For panel 2, long-term averages are computed from January 2006 to September 2022. EMs = emerging markets; GFSR = *Global Financial Stability Report*; IVOLCRUD = index of three-month, at-the-money implied volatility on oil options; LT Avg = long-term average; MOVE = yield-curve-weighted index of normalized implied volatility on one-month Treasury options; Q1, Q2, Q3 = first, second, and third quarters; USD = US dollars; VIX = Chicago Board Options Exchange Volatility Index; YTD = year to date.

Equity prices have fallen sharply and credit spreads have materially widened, as investors have aggressively pulled back from risk taking. Market liquidity has deteriorated markedly, including in benchmark sovereign bond markets. Cross-currency-basis swap spreads have also widened to their highest level since March 2020, in particular for the euro and the yen, reflecting the premium that investors have to pay to access dollar funding.

Overall, risk assets have performed very poorly in 2022 (Figure 1.2, panel 1). Emerging market assets have suffered large losses, partly reflecting the strength of the US dollar relative to most currencies, though with considerable heterogeneity. After declining in the summer, volatility has recently increased significantly across most asset classes. Rate volatility in particular has remained very elevated—at levels not witnessed since March 2020—reflecting the uncertainty about

the magnitude of the policy tightening and the economic outlook (Figure 1.2, panel 2).

Amid rising correlation with equities and poor market liquidity, crypto markets have seen extreme volatility (Figure 1.3, panel 1). Bitcoin lost over 50 percent of its value, some of the riskiest segments collapsed, and some crypto funds were unwound. During this period, Terra, the largest non-collateralized algorithmic stablecoin, experienced an investor run as its value fell below parity with the US dollar and eventually collapsed. Tether, the largest collateralized stablecoin, briefly traded below parity and saw significant outflows. By contrast, cash-backed and more transparent stablecoins received some inflows and were able to maintain parity during this volatile period (Figure 1.3, panel 2).

According to IMF staff models, the fall in equity prices has been driven by both rising rates and

Figure 1.3. Riskiest Segments of Crypto Markets Have Been Very Volatile

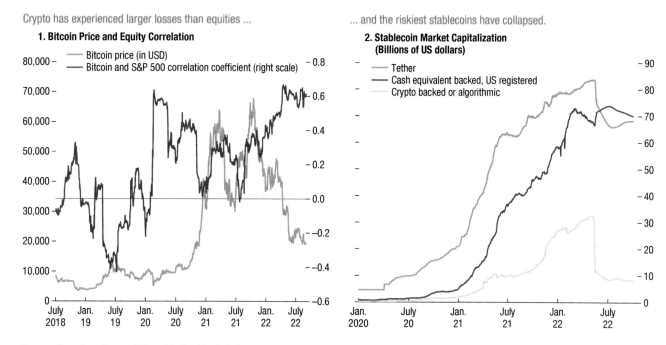

Crypto has experienced larger losses than equities ...

1. Bitcoin Price and Equity Correlation

... and the riskiest stablecoins have collapsed.

2. Stablecoin Market Capitalization (Billions of US dollars)

Sources: Bloomberg Finance L.P.; and IMF staff calculations.
Note: The correlation coefficient between the daily returns of Bitcoin and the S&P 500 are based on a 60-day moving average. SP500 = S&P 500; USD = US dollars.

expectations of lower earnings growth, in particular over the medium term (Figure 1.4, panel 1). Large firms have reported a contraction in profit margins due to higher costs, while downward revisions to global earnings growth forecasts appear to be gaining momentum on concerns about a possible recession. As central banks continue to normalize policy and the economic outlook deteriorates, and economic uncertainty rises, there is a risk of a further repricing in equity markets should investors require higher compensation to bear equity risk—as measured by equity risk premia. Risk premia in other risk asset markets would then also be expected to widen.

In credit markets, conditions have worsened and corporate bond spreads in advanced economies have been close to two-year highs, including for investment-grade bonds (Figure 1.4, panel 2). With corporate downgrades increasing, investors have grown increasingly concerned about an ensuing default cycle and pulled back from risk taking. As a result, access to credit has become more challenging, especially for sub-investment-grade firms. Reflecting higher government bond yields and wider credit spreads, corporate bond yields—the cost of new funding—have risen materially. Emerging market companies are particularly vulnerable as balance sheet leverage has risen since the

onset of the pandemic and could amplify losses during an economic slowdown.

Rising interest rates in advanced economies, coupled with intensifying global risk-off sentiment, have put significant pressure on sovereign spreads and borrowing costs in emerging markets. The effect has been especially severe for the more vulnerable economies. The spreads on foreign-currency debt for frontier markets (developing economies with less liquid bonds and only limited track records for bonds issuance) and other emerging markets with high-yield sovereign ratings have risen nearly to levels last seen at the peak of the pandemic sell-off in March 2020 (Figure 1.4, panel 3).[4] Despite the July tightening, spreads on the high-yield and frontier market sovereign indices are above 900 basis points (bps), approximately 500 bps higher than their pre-pandemic levels. Currently, 14 sovereigns have spreads exceeding 1,000 bps, a level at which they are commonly considered distressed and at high risk of default. Six more have already defaulted or engaged in debt restructuring (see the "Emerging Markets: Policy

[4]The frontier market classification comprises 43 countries that are included in the J.P. Morgan NEXGEM (Next Generation Markets) index or are low-income countries with international bond issuance that are not part of the index.

Figure 1.4. Markets Have Repriced Economic Risks

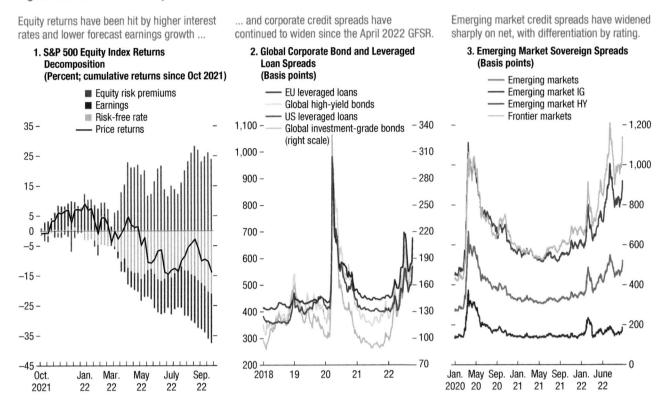

Equity returns have been hit by higher interest rates and lower forecast earnings growth ...

... and corporate credit spreads have continued to widen since the April 2022 GFSR.

Emerging market credit spreads have widened sharply on net, with differentiation by rating.

1. S&P 500 Equity Index Returns Decomposition
(Percent; cumulative returns since Oct 2021)

- Equity risk premiums
- Earnings
- Risk-free rate
- Price returns

2. Global Corporate Bond and Leveraged Loan Spreads
(Basis points)

- EU leveraged loans
- Global high-yield bonds
- US leveraged loans
- Global investment-grade bonds (right scale)

3. Emerging Market Sovereign Spreads
(Basis points)

- Emerging markets
- Emerging market IG
- Emerging market HY
- Frontier markets

Sources: Bloomberg L.P.; ICE Bond Indices; JPMorgan Chase & Co.; PitchBook Leveraged Commentary and Data; Refinitiv Datastream; and IMF staff calculations.
Note: In panel 1, lower equity risk premiums, lower risk-free rates, and higher earnings contribute positively to stock market returns, and vice versa. EU = European Union; GFSR = *Global Financial Stability Report*; HY = high yield; IG = investment grade; US = United States.

Space Continues to Erode" section).[5] By contrast, for many highly rated investment-grade sovereigns, which generally entered this tightening cycle in a stronger position, spreads have remained within a tight range, widening only modestly, on net, this year.

Large currency depreciations against the US dollar in some jurisdictions, particularly in Europe and Japan, have partly tracked widening interest rate differentials related to the faster pace of rate hikes by the Federal Reserve (Figure 1.5, panel 1) and, in the case of Europe, also mounting concerns about growth prospects.[6] Outside of Latin America, which benefited from proactively raising rates in 2021 and from the earlier rise in commodity prices, emerging market currencies have broadly depreciated this year.

They have been pressured by higher rates in the United States and, more recently, increased fears of recession and lower commodity prices (Figure 1.5, panel 2). The ongoing US dollar appreciation presents a challenge for both advanced and emerging central banks. Several have resorted to intervention in the foreign exchange market (Chile, Czech Republic, Indonesia, Japan, Philippines, and Malaysia, among others), or have signaled their readiness to do so, with the objective of limiting currency volatility and the impact on inflation from higher import prices.

European financial markets have shown significant strains, reflecting the unprecedented energy crisis triggered by Russia's war in Ukraine, continued supply chain disruptions, and heightened concerns about the economic outlook.[7] Since the April 2022 GFSR, asset prices have sold off sharply and energy prices have reached record-high levels in the summer as a

[5]The six countries are Belarus, Lebanon, Sri Lanka, Suriname, Russia, and Zambia. On August 10, 2022, Ukraine's foreign creditors (for example, bondholders) backed its request for a two-year freeze (deferral) on debt service payments.

[6]Japan's worsening external balance is another factor cited by some market participants.

[7]See the "Commodities Special Feature" in Chapter 1 of the October 2022 WEO.

Figure 1.5. Currencies Have Experienced Large Moves in Advanced Economies and Emerging Markets

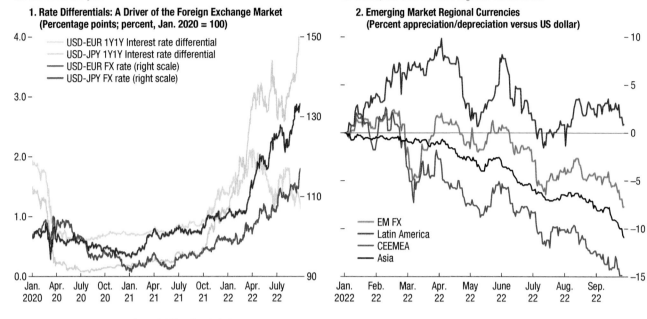

Interest rate differentials are a key driver of recent depreciation of the euro and the yen.

Emerging market currencies have also depreciated against the US dollar, but with marked regional differences.

Sources: Bloomberg Finance L.P.; and IMF staff calculations.
Note: Panel 2 is the regional median. Asia comprises India, Indonesia, Malaysia, Pakistan, the Philippines, and Thailand. CEEMEA comprises Hungary, Morocco, Poland, Romania, and South Africa. Latin America comprises Brazil, Chile, Colombia, Mexico, and Peru. 1Y1Y = one-year, one-year forward; CEEMEA = central and eastern Europe, Middle East, and Africa; EM = emerging market; EUR = euro; FX = foreign exchange; JPY = Japanese yen; USD = US dollar.

result of disruptions in natural gas supplies from Russia (Figure 1.6, panel 1). The large swings in gas and electricity prices have also raised concerns about the funding conditions and possible cash shortages at some European utility companies. Skyrocketing energy prices and high volatility have led to large margin calls on derivatives positions used by utilities to lock in future electricity price sales. As a result, companies have to post extra collateral to maintain their positions—a development that appears to have contributed to a widening of government bond swap spreads in the euro area (Figure 1.6, panel 1, black line). Concerns over short-term liquidity of energy utilities have prompted several European governments to implement emergency support schemes in the form of short-term liquidity line and loan guarantees, while measures such as freezing energy bills were also implemented to support households and energy-intensive businesses.[8]

In the euro area, with the European Central Bank (ECB) starting to normalize policy, concerns about

fragmentation risk have resurfaced, as investors have focused on fiscal vulnerabilities in some member states. Spreads of southern European government bond yields over (similar-maturity) German yields have widened, on net, since April. However, the ECB's active use of its asset reinvestment policy and the announcement of the new "Transmission Protection Instrument" designed to ensure a smooth transmission of monetary policy, have helped so far contain a disorderly widening of spreads (Figure 1.6, panel 2; Box 1.2).

In the UK, investor concerns about the fiscal and inflation outlook after the announcement of large debt-financed tax cuts and fiscal measures to deal with high energy prices weighed heavily on market sentiment in late September. Amid high market volatility, the British pound depreciated abruptly, while yields on UK sovereign bonds rose sharply (Figure 1.6, panels 3 and 4). The scale and speed of yield increases, especially at the long end of the curve, reportedly had a significant impact on levered positions held by UK institutional investors, particularly pension funds. Large mark-to-market losses and associated margin calls raised the specter of pernicious fire sales and

---

[8]Several European countries have set up new schemes to provide liquidity support for energy companies, including Finland, Germany, Sweden, and the United Kingdom. The United Kingdom also introduced the Energy Price Guarantee to limit energy prices.

Figure 1.6. The European Energy Crisis Is Deepening amid Growing Investor Concerns about Fragmentation Risk in the EU and Fiscal Concerns in the UK

Energy prices in Europe have skyrocketed ...

1. European Energy Prices (One-Year Forward) and Euro Area Swap Spreads
(Index: Jan. 2022 = 100; basis points)

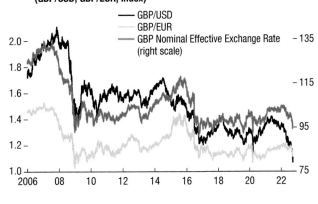

... while investor concerns about fragmentation risk have resurfaced.

2. German 10-Year Yields and Sovereign Spread
(Basis points; percent)

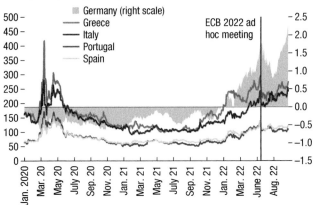

The pound depreciated sharply amid concerns over fiscal deterioration and higher inflation ...

3. The Pound Exchange Rate
(GBP/USD, GBP/EUR; index)

... and yields on UK sovereign debt rose sharply and the curve inverted.

4. UK Gilt Yields
(Percent, basis points)

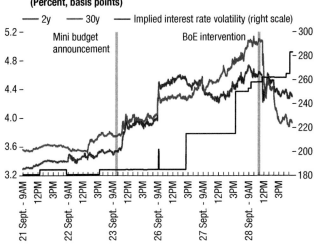

Sources: Bloomberg Finance L.P.; IMF GDS database; and IMF staff calculations.
Note: In panel 3, swap spread shows the difference between the 2-y swap rate and German bond yield of the same maturity. BoE = Bank of England; ECB = European Central Bank. An effective exchange rate (also known as a trade-weighted exchange rate) is a weighted average of the individual exchange rates of a particular country with its main trading partners. The bilateral exchange rates are weighted according to the importance of each partner country's share of trade with the reporting country. In panel 4, the implied interest rate volatility is the GBP 3 month 10 year swaption implied volatility.

self-fulfilling price dynamics—causing yields to rise further. To prevent dysfunction in the gilt market from posing a material risk to UK financial stability, the Bank of England, in line with its financial stability mandate, announced on September 28 temporary and targeted purchases of long-dated UK government bonds. It also indicated that purchases, scheduled to end on October 14, would be unwound in a smooth and orderly fashion once risks to market functioning were judged to have subsided. In addition, to reiterate that these purchases were made purely on financial stability grounds, the Bank of England noted that it would not hesitate to hike interest rates by as much as needed to achieve its 2 percent target in the medium term. Following the announcement, the British pound appreciated while yields on UK government debt reversed a portion of their earlier increases, particularly at the long end. Advanced economies' yields also fell in sympathy, in line with the recent elevated correlations. Anticipating that policymakers will have to tighten more to counter the inflationary consequences of the announced fiscal measures, investors have repriced the expected path of UK monetary policy. They now expect the Bank of England to hike the policy rate by about 240 basis points by year end, bringing it to nearly 6 percent in 2023.

With investors aggressively pulling back from risk taking recently as they reassess their economic and policy outlook, there is a danger of a disorderly repricing of risk. In particular, volatility and a sudden tightening in financial conditions could interact with, and be amplified by, preexisting financial vulnerabilities—including those that have emerged since the pandemic. The IMF staff's indicator-based framework shows that balance sheet vulnerabilities are currently most prominent in the sovereign sector (Box 1.1, Figure 1.1.1). In most jurisdictions, the public sector has cushioned some of the impact of the pandemic shock on the balance sheets of households and nonfinancial firms at the cost of deterioration of the fiscal position and a large increase in sovereign debt. In addition, balance sheet vulnerabilities are elevated in the nonbank financial intermediation sector, reflecting high liquidity and maturity transformation—and exposure to credit and duration risk—as well as interconnectivity with the banking sector. In the nonfinancial corporate sector, vulnerabilities have declined as large firms have benefited from easy financing conditions and ample liquidity (especially in the United States), but some sectors and lower-rated firms have started to see a deterioration in conditions and a pickup in credit rating downgrades that could presage a rise in default rates from below-average levels. In the housing sector, vulnerabilities remain elevated in emerging markets and some advanced economies; the house-price-to-income ratio has reached its highest level in two decades in many countries at a time of rising mortgage rates and tighter lending standards (for more details, see the "Housing Markets: At a Tipping Point?" section).

The significant worsening in market liquidity experienced across asset classes is another important source of fragility and potential shock amplifier (see Figure 1.17). Poor market liquidity conditions reflect both fundamental and technical factors (for details, see the "Poor Market Liquidity: A Shock Amplifier" section). Market liquidity has deteriorated even in

typically highly liquid markets, such as advanced economy government bond markets, and conditions have become more challenging even in more standardized and exchange-traded products, such as stocks, foreign exchange, and exchange-traded futures.

Against a backdrop of tighter financial conditions and extraordinary uncertainty about the outlook, global economic growth for 2022 has been marked down to 3.2 percent, 0.4 percentage point lower than projected in the April 2022 WEO. As a result, the balance of risks is squarely skewed to the downside, and global financial stability risks have materially worsened since the April 2022 GFSR (Figure 1.7, panel 1). The IMF growth-at-risk framework indicates that downside risks are very high compared to historical norms (Figure 1.7, panel 2). The probability of growth falling below zero is currently about 10 percent for 2022.

Advanced Economies: Central Banks Still Aiming for a Smooth Landing

Many central banks in advanced economies have accelerated their pace of tightening since the April 2022 GFSR to prevent inflationary pressures from becoming entrenched and avoid a de-anchoring of inflation expectations. Some have tightened aggressively and may have to continue to do so—possibly even more than currently priced in markets—to bring inflation credibly back to target.

Since the April 2022 GFSR, the Federal Reserve has initiated the process of balance sheet reduction (quantitative tightening) and raised the target range for the federal funds rate by 275 basis points—including three 75 basis point increases, a magnitude not seen since 1994. The ECB has ended its net asset purchases, raised its key policy rates by 125 basis points (after eight years of negative rates on the deposit facility), and designed a new tool to prevent fragmentation in the euro area. The Bank of England also announced that it will reduce its gilts holding held in the Asset Purchase Facility (APF) by 80 billion pounds over the next 12 months.[9] Active sales of gilts via auction, originally

---

[9]The Bank of England set its gilt sales auction schedule on a quarterly basis. The bank will hold short, medium, and long-term auctions and announced it plans to sell GBP580MM per auction in each of these buckets. See Market Notice setting out the schedule for the gilt sales operations for Q4 2022: https://www.bankofengland .co.uk/markets/market-notices/2022/september/apf-gilt-sales -22-september.

Figure 1.7. Global Growth-at-Risk

Risks to growth are squarely skewed to the downside ...

... and high compared with historical norms.

1. Near-Term Growth Forecast Densities
(Probability density)

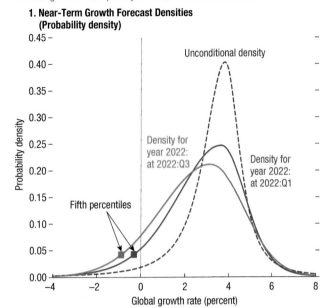

2. Near-Term Growth-at-Risk Forecasts
(Percentile rank)

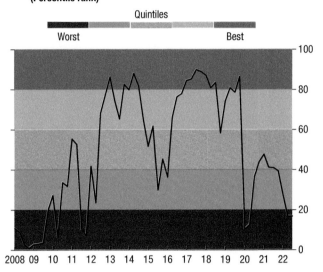

Sources: Bank for International Settlements; Bloomberg Finance L.P.; Haver Analytics; IMF, International Financial Statistics database; and IMF staff calculations.
Note: Forecast density estimates are centered around the IMF *World Economic Outlook* (WEO) forecasts for 2022, as of 2022:Q1 and 2022:Q3, respectively. The latter reflects the current available estimate of the third quarter forecast for 2022. To gauge downside risks over time, in panel 2, the black line traces the evolution of the 5th percentile threshold (the growth-at-risk metric) of near-term growth forecast densities. The color of the shading depicts the percentile rank for the growth-at-risk metric, from 1991 onward. See the April 2018 *Global Financial Stability Report* for details.

scheduled to commence on October 3, 2022, have been postponed to October 31 following the Bank of England's announcement on September 28 of temporary and targeted purchases of long-dated UK government bonds. Given the uncertain growth and inflation outlook, the Federal Reserve, the ECB, and the Reserve Bank of Australia have indicated that they would no longer provide precise forward policy guidance about the expected path of policy, moving instead to a meeting-by-meeting approach based on incoming data. Several other central banks in advanced economies—including the Bank of England, Bank of Canada, Reserve Bank of New Zealand, and Swiss National Bank—have also taken significant steps toward policy normalization.

Reflecting the more aggressive tightening stance, the near-term market-implied expected path of policy rates has shifted higher in most advanced economies since the April GFSR (Figure 1.8, panel 1). With investors frequently reassessing their economic and policy outlook based on incoming data, medium- and long-term interest rates have been quite volatile, ending the period higher in some countries (Figure 1.8, panel 2).

Real yields have risen markedly, driven by a combination of a higher expected path of short-term real rates (as measured by the risk-adjusted real yield) and, to some extent, rising real term premiums.[10] Rising real term premiums point to greater uncertainty about the path of policy and the growth outlook. Meanwhile, inflation breakevens (market-implied proxies for future inflation) have generally declined across tenors. In the euro area and the United Kingdom, after declining midyear, five-year breakevens rose sharply in August as the energy crisis intensified. However, breakevens have come down recently in both regions.

Evidence based on inflation options suggests that investors are assigning significant probability to inflation outcomes being greater than 3 percent in coming years, particularly in the euro area and the United Kingdom (Figure 1.9, panel 1). However, disagreement among investors around the most likely outcomes appears to be more notable than it was at the end of last year. In the case of the United States

---

[10]For details on the underlying yield-curve-decomposition methodology applied here, see Goel and Malik (2021).

Figure 1.8. Drivers of Advanced Economy Bond Yields

Market-implied expectations of policy rates have risen since the previous GFSR.

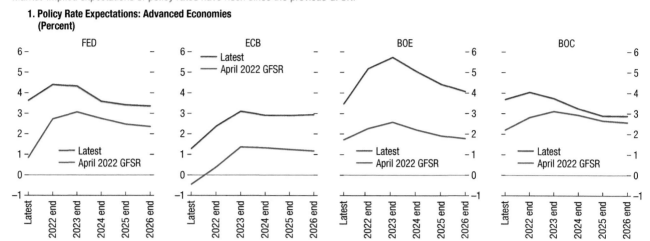

1. Policy Rate Expectations: Advanced Economies
  (Percent)

Medium- and long-term rates have increased notably, driven by higher yields.

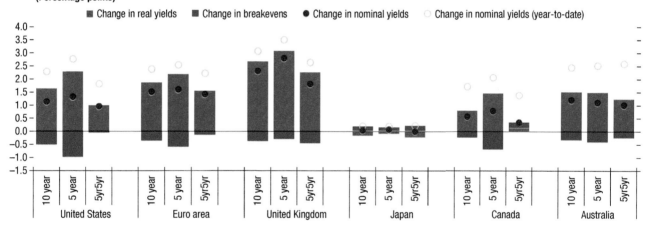

2. Change in Yields since the April 2022 GFSR
  (Percentage points)

Sources: Bloomberg Finance L.P.; and IMF staff calculations.
Note: 5yr5yr = five-year, five-year forward; BOC = Bank of Canada; BOE = Bank of England; ECB = European Central Bank; FED = Federal Reserve; GFSR = *Global Financial Stability Report.*

and the euro area, there are now meaningful odds of both low- and high-inflation outcomes—likely a consequence of greater concern about a slowdown in aggregate growth (Figure 1.9).[11]

Fears that central banks may be raising policy rates well above neutral levels to tackle inflationary

pressures have raised investor concerns about a possible recession in advanced economies. In the United States, for example, the median September 2022 Federal Open Market Committee (FOMC) participant anticipates the federal funds rate to significantly exceed the FOMC projection of the nominal neutral rate over the entire forecast period (Figure 1.10, panel 1). In real terms, the federal funds rate is expected to climb from deeply negative levels in 2022 to more than 150 basis points in 2023, well above the neutral real rate—nearly 300 basis points of real policy tightening (Figure 1.10, panel 2).

[11]In the euro area, survey-based measures suggest that consumers are more concerned about high inflation, pointing to a risk of expectations de-anchoring. See ECB Consumer Expectations Survey and I. Schnabel's speech in Jackson Hole, "Monetary Policy and the Great Volatility," which can be found at https://www.ecb.europa.eu/press/key/date/2022/html/ecb.sp220827-93f7d07535.en.html.

Figure 1.9. Market-Implied Probability of Future Inflation Outcomes

The probability of high-inflation outcomes remains significant, especially in the euro area and UK ...

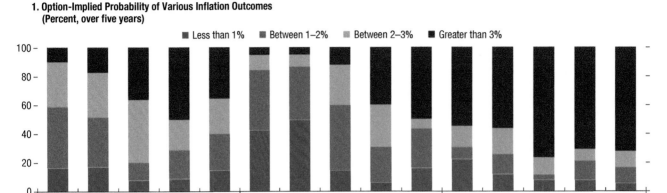

1. Option-Implied Probability of Various Inflation Outcomes
(Percent, over five years)

■ Less than 1%   ■ Between 1–2%   ■ Between 2–3%   ■ Greater than 3%

... but with notable disagreement among investors.

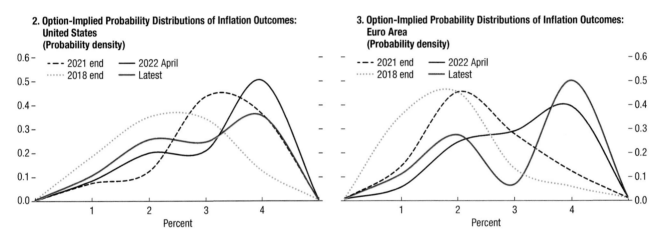

2. Option-Implied Probability Distributions of Inflation Outcomes:
United States
(Probability density)

3. Option-Implied Probability Distributions of Inflation Outcomes:
Euro Area
(Probability density)

Sources: Bloomberg Finance L.P.; and IMF staff calculations.
Note: "Latest" refers to the time of the October 2022 GFSR. Probabilities in panel 1 are derived from inflation caps and floors. GFSR = *Global Financial Stability Report*.

Such recession fears may well be justified based on historical evidence. Every time the Federal Reserve has raised the federal funds rate close to, or above, measures of the neutral nominal rate, the US economy has entered a recession soon thereafter (Figure 1.11). The only exception over the past four decades was the tightening cycle in 1994, perhaps in part because inflation was not excessively high around this period—when considered within a long-term historical context—and because the policy rate was cut within a year following the peak of the tightening cycle (see Box 1.3 for a discussion of how US rates and other financial variables behaved during previous tightening cycles).

Emerging Markets: Policy Space Continues to Erode

Emerging market and frontier market central banks have also continued to tighten monetary policy, but regional differences remain significant. Latin American central banks have been more proactive, hiking policy rates earlier and more aggressively in response to inflationary pressures. Central banks in central and eastern Europe began tightening policy later and at a slower pace initially, contributing to investor concerns about high inflation and weaker regional currencies, although they have subsequently accelerated the hiking cycle. Türkiye is a notable outlier: the central bank

Figure 1.10. Policy Rates versus Neutral Levels

The assessment by the Federal Open Market Committee (FOMC) of appropriate monetary policy has shifted higher, with the federal funds rate expected to possibly exceed the current projection of the neutral rate over the forecast period.

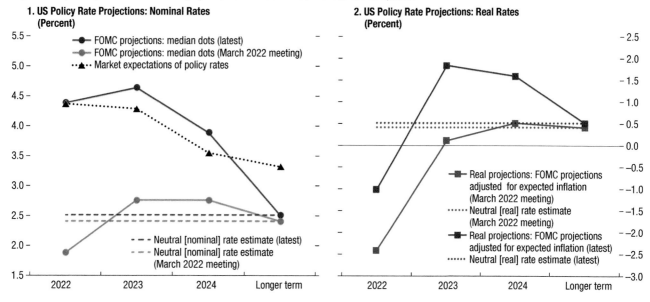

Sources: Bloomberg Finance L.P.; Federal Reserve; and IMF staff calculations.

has continued to cut rates despite rising inflation and ongoing currency weakness. Reflecting an initially more benign inflation outlook, Asian central banks have started to hike rates only recently and more modestly relative to their emerging market peers. Markets are pricing in an end to rate hikes in most countries by the end of this year or early next year (excluding Asia) and substantial rate cuts by some emerging market central banks in 2023 (Figure 1.12, panel 1).

Conditions in local currency bond markets have worsened materially in many emerging and frontier markets, reflecting concerns about the macroeconomic outlook and policy credibility, as well as deterioration in the fiscal position since the pandemic. Sovereign bond term premiums have increased sharply, especially for central and eastern Europe (Figure 1.12, panel 2). Term premiums tend to rise when domestic central banks tighten, but the size and speed of increases in some markets have taken investors by surprise, especially as US term premiums have been relatively stable. Volatility in local bond market yields has also risen globally and has approached peak historical levels in some emerging markets (Figure 1.12, panel 3). Tensions in domestic bond markets are likely to persist, especially as rising US real policy rates compress

rate differentials and pressure emerging market central banks (Figure 1.12, panel 4). Expected policy easing may be difficult to deliver if advanced economy central banks hike rates more than expected or keep policy rates higher for longer.

Tight Conditions Are Squeezing the Most Vulnerable Emerging Markets

Emerging markets face a multitude of risks stemming from high external borrowing costs, stubbornly high inflation, volatile commodity markets, heightened uncertainty about the global economic outlook and the war in Ukraine, and pressures from policy tightening in advanced economies. So far, investors have continued to differentiate across emerging market economies; unlike in previous crisis episodes, many of the largest emerging markets seem to be more resilient to external vulnerabilities and classic balance of payments shocks. Many frontier markets, however, are facing potential loss of market access and a high probability of sovereign default, and more than half of all low-income countries are judged by the IMF to be already in, or to have a high probability of entering, debt distress.

Figure 1.11. Monetary Policy Tightening and Recessions: A 60-Year Record

Historically, each time the Federal Reserve has raised the federal funds rate close to, or above, the neutral nominal rate, the US economy has entered a recession soon thereafter.

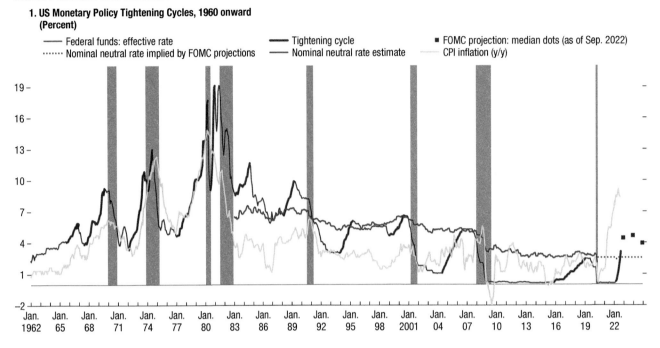

1. US Monetary Policy Tightening Cycles, 1960 onward
(Percent)

- Federal funds: effective rate
- Tightening cycle
- FOMC projection: median dots (as of Sep. 2022)
- Nominal neutral rate implied by FOMC projections
- Nominal neutral rate estimate
- CPI inflation (y/y)

Sources: Bloomberg Finance L.P.; Federal Reserve; US Bureau of Labor Statistics; and IMF staff calculations.
Note: Measurement of the neutral rate is subject to uncertainty, with different approaches proposed in the literature; see for example, Aronovich and Meldrum (2020, 2021), Kiley (2020), Del Negro and others (2017), and Johannsen and Mertens (2016). The nominal neutral rate estimate shown here is constructed based on the real neutral rate measure proposed by Holston, Laubach, and Williams (2017), in which the former is equal to the real neutral rate plus inflation expectations. The inflation expectations series used here—corresponding to the five-year, five-year forward horizon—is published by the Federal Reserve Board going back to the mid-1980s and is based on the model by D'Amico, Kim, and Wei (2018). Gray shaded areas indicate National Bureau of Economic Research recession periods. Consumer price inflation (CPI) corresponds to headline inflation (urban consumers). FOMC = Federal Open Market Committee; y/y = year over year.

In addition, there is a growing risk that authorities in advanced economies will respond to concerns about supply chain vulnerabilities by adopting more inward-looking policies. A disorderly restructuring of global supply chains—involving higher trade barriers and increased uncertainty about trade policy—would undermine a key engine of growth for emerging markets, amplify macroeconomic and capital flow volatility, and reduce emerging markets' access to international capital markets.[12]

Local currency bond markets have seen large net *portfolio outflows* from nonresident investors this year, reflecting continuing pessimism about the outlook for emerging market sovereign bonds. Despite a modest rebound in August, sentiment appeared to deteriorate again in September. Equity flows are down moderately for 2022 on net, with India in particular

partially reversing some of the large outflows seen in previous months in August (Figure 1.13, panel 1). In China, investors withdrew about $75 billion from local currency bonds between February and August 2022, including nearly 15 percent of foreign holdings of government bonds, but still a small share of the overall bond market.[13] The compression of yield differentials, largely due to diverging monetary policy, has likely been the primary driver of outflows from China, although the rise of benchmark-driven investors may also be playing a supporting role.[14] Taking a longer view, nonresident portfolio flows into local currency debt for emerging markets excluding China have been stagnant in recent years, a trend

[13]This figure includes Chinese government bonds, policy bank bonds, corporate and bank bonds, and asset-backed securities, though foreign holdings are primarily concentrated in government and policy bank bonds.

[14]Arslanalp and others (2020).

[12]See Gopinath (2022).

Figure 1.12. Monetary Policy Outlook and Local Bond Markets in Emerging Markets

Market pricing suggests differences in tightening cycles across emerging markets will persist ...

1. Historical and Market-Implied Policy Rates across Regions
(Percent)

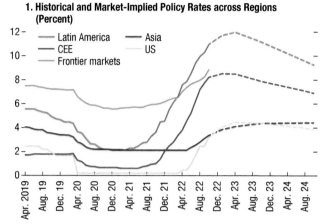

... while term premiums have increased sharply in some regions.

2. Change in Five-Year Term Premiums since January 2020
(Basis points)

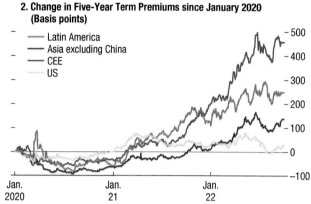

Local bond markets in some countries have been unusually volatile ...

3. Standard Deviation of 20-Day Moving Average in Emerging Market Local Yields
(Basis points)

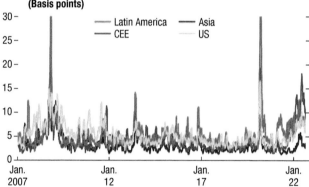

... particularly as rapidly rising US real rates put pressure on emerging market markets to respond.

4. Short-Term Real Rates
(Ex ante one-year rates, percent)

Sources: Bloomberg Finance L.P.; BNP Paribas; Consensus Forecasts; and IMF staff calculations.
Note: Panel 3 uses local currency yields from the JPMorgan Government Bond Index–Emerging Markets (GBI-EM) for emerging markets and the 10-year US Treasury yield for the United States. In panel 4, the ex ante median rate in a region is calculated as the one-year-ahead forward rate minus the Bloomberg consensus for inflation in the year ahead. CEE = central and eastern Europe; US = United States.

exacerbated by the COVID-19 shock (Figure 1.13, panel 2).[15] Recent outflows account for only a relatively small fraction of accumulated inflows over the past decade.

Regarding *investment fund* flows, bond funds dedicated to emerging markets (hard and local currency combined) have seen record dollar outflows of over $60 billion[16] through late-September 2022, nearly 10 percent of assets under management

(Figure 1.13, panel 3).[17] However, when measured on an assets under management-adjusted basis, these outflows have still been lower than during past episodes of distress such as the 2013 taper tantrum episode. China-dedicated funds also account for a significantly larger share of the asset class in 2022 compared to

---

[15]The sample comprises 24 emerging markets excluding China.
[16]This figure relies only on weekly reported fund data from EPFR.

[17]Portfolio flows represent cross-border transactions in local markets. By contrast, fund flows capture retail and institutional investors buying and selling hard and local currency funds focused on emerging markets, which gives an indication of market demand but may or may not have implications for the capital account. Fund flow data also include some domestically domiciled local currency funds.

Figure 1.13. Emerging Market Portfolio Flows, New Issues, and Market Pricing

Local currency bond outflows have been substantial in 2022, while equity outflows have been modest.

Recent outflows have been relatively small compared to the overall stock of foreign holdings.

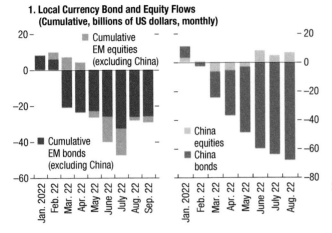

1. Local Currency Bond and Equity Flows
(Cumulative, billions of US dollars, monthly)

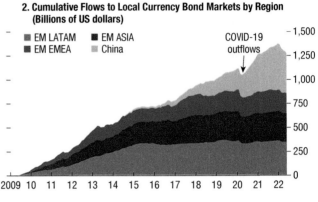

2. Cumulative Flows to Local Currency Bond Markets by Region
(Billions of US dollars)

Bond funds dedicated to emerging markets have seen large outflows reach nearly 10 percent of assets under management, which still compares somewhat favorably to the draw-downs in 2013 and 2015.

Capital flows at risk have deteriorated since April 2022 amid persistent dollar strength, with over a 40 percent implied probability of outflows.

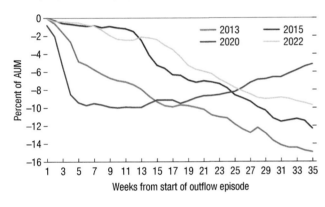

3. Emerging Market Bond Fund Flow Episodes
(Percent of AUM, by cycle)

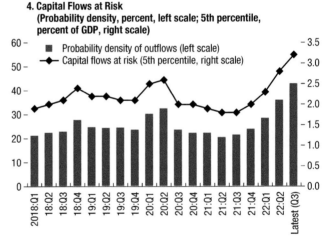

4. Capital Flows at Risk
(Probability density, percent, left scale; 5th percentile, percent of GDP, right scale)

Sources: Bloomberg Finance L.P.; EPFR; national sources; and IMF staff calculations.
Note: Panel 1 includes primarily local currency government bonds. Chinese data includes primarily government and policy bank bonds, as well as some corporate, bank, and asset backed securities. Panel 3 refers only to weekly reported fund data from EPFR. Chinese figures are Chinese government and policy bank bonds. AUM = assets under management; EM = emerging market; EMEA = Europe, Middle East, and Africa; LATAM = Latin America and the Caribbean.

previous years and have had relatively greater outflows so far this year.

Fixed-income liquidity has been particularly challenging in emerging and frontier markets. Market participants have reported that these conditions are driven primarily by high economic and policy uncertainty, as well as by the large number of deeply discounted sovereign debt issuances where liquidity is typically poor. Liquidity in the emerging market credit default swap index of major sovereigns has apparently been

an exception: investors have reportedly been using these instruments to adjust their aggregate exposure when individual bonds are difficult to source at scale.

Issuance of sovereign hard currency bonds has deteriorated to its slowest pace since 2015 so far this year. From January through September 2022, the volume of sovereign new issues declined 54 percent year over year, to $68 billion, with substantial issuance concessions (that is, premiums higher than those on existing benchmark bonds), even for higher-rated issuers.

The weighted-average maturity of new issuance has declined, with only 18 percent of bonds issued at maturities of more than 15 years—the lowest since 2013. Corporate nonfinancial bond issuance declined to just under $60 billion over the same period, down 75 percent year over year. Issuance conditions continued to be very challenging in September in what is normally a busy month.

Downside risks to portfolio flows remain elevated compared to historical norms amid persistent dollar strength, market volatility, and heightened uncertainty about the economic and political outlook. IMF staff analysis, based on the capital-flows-at-risk methodology (see the April 2020 GFSR), suggests that the probability of outflows over the next three quarters (including the current quarter) has risen to over 40 percent, up from 30 percent in the April 2022 GFSR (see Figure 1.13, panel 4). Capital flows at risk, defined as the lowest fifth percentile of the forward-looking distribution for capital flows, have increased to 3.2 percent of GDP for emerging markets.

Emerging and frontier markets face heightened fiscal vulnerabilities and uncertain growth prospects, leaving many countries exposed to renewed market volatility. Inflation has risen to multiyear highs and is anticipated to remain elevated into 2023, contributing to ongoing policy and economic challenges. While fundamentals have improved since the depth of the COVID-19 shock, budget deficits remain at the upper end of historical ranges, growth is slowing heading into 2023, and a rapid return to pre-pandemic debt dynamics could be difficult. Current account deficits also have widened sharply in several emerging and frontier markets, though the effects of higher oil prices and divergent recoveries on external balances continue to be heterogenous (Figure 1.14, panel 1).

Public debt burdens have increased markedly across most emerging and frontier markets in recent years, eroding necessary fiscal buffers to mitigate new shocks and pushing up refinancing risks. On average, the ratio of public debt to GDP in emerging markets has increased from 36 percent in 2012 to over 60 percent in 2022. However, the features of this increased vulnerability vary considerably by country type. Frontier markets have relied more on foreign currency borrowing, making them more directly susceptible to tightening financial conditions in advanced economies. By contrast, many larger and more developed emerging markets have been able to shift toward increased local currency financing, particularly in recent years (Figure 1.14, panel 2). A developed local currency bond market can help mitigate currency risk, often a source of distress in emerging market crises; facilitate stronger fiscal capacity; and support effective monetary policy transmission (IMF 2021).

Foreign reserves buffers are generally healthy in most emerging markets, having increased substantially from the lows seen during previous periods of emerging market distress (Figure 1.14, panel 3).[18] However, a vulnerable tail persists, with the 25th percentile of countries remaining well below the recommended level of reserves adequacy. While weak reserves buffers are more prominent among frontier markets, a few larger and more developed emerging markets have seen reserves come under pressure recently.

Against this backdrop, external funding conditions are now extremely challenging for many lower-rated issuers and, under a severe downside scenario, debt distress could spread to more countries. IMF staff analysis based on historical sensitivities suggests that, should global financial conditions tighten sharply from current levels, the number of distressed sovereigns (with spreads of more than 1,000 basis points) could rise from 20 to 31.[19] Moreover, over 40 countries (including half the countries in the emerging market bond index) would have spreads exceeding 700 basis points, a level at which issuance has been very challenging historically. Given that most frontier markets started issuing foreign-exchange-denominated bonds only after 2010, they have limited experience with rolling over maturities in adverse market conditions. However systemic risks are limited, as even in the stress scenario distressed issuers would account for only 20 percent of the benchmark emerging market bond index (based on market capitalization) and barely 5 percent of global GDP. Spreads would remain below 600 basis points for more than 60 percent of the index, illustrating the bifurcated nature of the asset class (Figure 1.14, panel 4).

Importantly, the rise in local currency issuance in more developed emerging markets has been largely

[18]Reserves are measured by the IMF's Assessing Reserve Adequacy metric.

[19]The downside shock includes a 200 basis point shock to US BBB spreads and reflects historical sensitivities of emerging market credit spreads estimated in the asset valuation model presented in the October 2019 GFSR. Index weights are based on the JPMorgan EMBI Global Diversified Index.

Figure 1.14. Emerging Market Vulnerabilities

Weak growth and high fiscal deficits could pose headwinds for emerging market financial assets.

1. Macroeconomic Indicators
(Percentile rank since 2000 of EM median, by year)

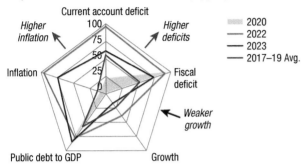

Larger emerging markets have been able to issue more local currency debt, while frontier markets have relied more on foreign currency debt.

2. Change in Public Debt by Currency, 2012–22
(Percentage points of GDP)

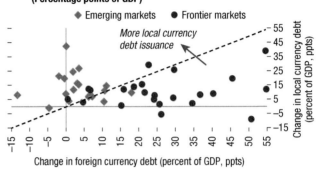

While reserves appear generally healthy, buffers have eroded and a weak tail of countries persists.

3. Reserve Adequacy: Reserves as a Share of the IMF's Assessing Reserve Adequacy Metric
(Percent, 2010–22 range)

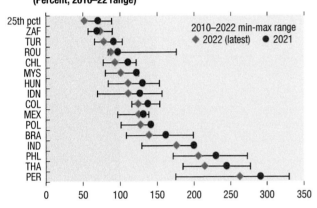

In these circumstances, many frontier markets face poor prospects for market access, with the potential for debt distress to spread if conditions worsen.

4. Emerging Market Sovereign Bond Spreads, Distribution and Downside Scenario
(Index weight, left scale; number of countries, right scale)

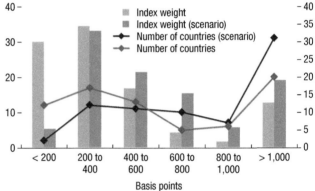

Foreign participation in local currency debt markets has declined, providing some insulation from shifts in external risk sentiment.

5. Foreign Share of Local Currency Debt
(Percent share)

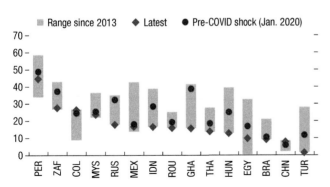

Domestic local currency yields have surged to the highest in a decade, but adjusted for inflation, the rise appears more manageable.

6. Local Currency Yields, Adjusted by One-Year-Ahead Inflation Expectations, Distribution
(Share of countries by yield, median)

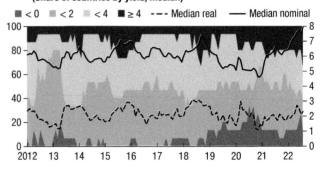

Sources: Bloomberg Finance, L.P.; Bondradar; EPFR; JPMorgan Chase & Co.; national sources; IMF, World Economic Outlook database; and IMF staff calculations.
Note: Panel 1 comprises 80 emerging market and developing economies. In panel 3, reserves in the range of 100–150 percent of the ARA metric are considered broadly adequate for precautionary purposes, though country specific considerations may apply. Panel 3 is based on 10-year zero coupon yields. In panels 3 and 5, data labels use International Organization for Standardization (ISO) country codes. EMs = emerging markets; pctl = percentile; ppts = percentage points.

absorbed by domestic investors as banks and non-bank financial institutions have taken on an increased financing burden. This has been particularly true since the COVID-19 shock, as most local currency debt markets did not experience the surge of inflows seen ahead of past episodes of emerging market stress (for example, 2013, 2015), providing some resilience against the confluence of shocks in 2022.[20] Continuing a trend evident since the mid-2010s, the nonresident share of local debt has declined in several large emerging markets by at least 10 percentage points since January 2020 (Figure 1.14, panel 5).

While exposure to external investors has declined somewhat and has been a source of resilience, the financing burden has shifted to the domestic market, with the sovereign bank nexus emerging as a key vulnerability (see Chapter 2 of the April 2022 GFSR). However, while nominal rates have risen sharply to the highest in a decade, on a real basis financing costs appear more manageable for core emerging markets despite a material rise over the past year (Figure 1.14, panel 6).

Many Frontier Markets Could Face Defaults and Difficult Restructuring

Challenges facing frontier markets are driven by a combination of tightening financial conditions, deteriorating fundamentals, and high exposure to commodity price volatility. The median debt-to-GDP ratio for frontier markets has nearly doubled since 2010, although it is expected to decline somewhat in 2022. Interest expenses on government debt have continued to rise, increasing immediate liquidity pressures and potentially negative policy consequences, such as crowding out of public investment. Credible medium-term fiscal consolidation plans are paramount to easing domestic refinancing costs and restoring international market access (Figure 1.15, panel 1). Despite the midyear drop on rising fears of recession, commodity prices (in particular for oil and metals) remain higher than pre-pandemic levels. While this has further weakened the macroeconomic outlook for importers, many frontier markets are commodity exporters and

have benefited from higher prices. Conversely, the rise in global food prices is adding to vulnerabilities in frontier markets by increasing the policy trade-offs: higher inflation calls for tighter monetary policy, but supporting the most vulnerable would require additional fiscal space or expenditure reprioritization.

In an environment of poor fundamentals and lack of investor risk appetite, defaults may follow. Frontier issuance has dropped sharply in 2022, with total volume down 75 percent through September and only three issuances since early April (Figure 1.15, panel 2). Market access for frontier markets has deteriorated sharply just as rollover needs are set to increase substantially in the next two to three years. Over 40 percent of frontier bonds maturing through 2025 are trading at distressed spreads (above 1,000 basis points), and close to 80 percent are trading at spreads of more than 700 basis points (Figure 1.15, panel 3). Without a substantial improvement in market conditions, many of these issuers may have to seek alternatives such as new bilateral or multilateral financing, including IMF-supported programs, or debt reprofiling and restructuring, in addition to structural reforms to improve fiscal balances.

If frontier markets end up in default, an increasingly complex creditor base, combined with gaps in the international architecture for resolving sovereign debt, could lead to long and difficult debt negotiations among a wide variety of creditors, further delaying market access and raising the costs of financial distress (IMF 2020). Even in the absence of outright default, a prolonged period of high borrowing rates could lead to heightened policy uncertainty and debt overhang for years to come. Frontier markets have increasingly come to rely on private sector creditors (Eurobonds and syndicated loans), and the number of their bilateral and multilateral creditors has also increased. Several countries that have traded at distressed levels in recent months, or that are already in default, owe more than one-third of their external debt to the private sector (Figure 1.15, panel 4). Of the four frontier markets currently in default (Belarus, Sri Lanka, Suriname, Zambia), both Suriname and Zambia have been in protracted negotiations, with discussions complicated by the wide variety of creditors, commodity price volatility, and large uncertainties regarding future government revenues. The recent default in Sri Lanka, which has triggered popular unrest, could face similar challenges. In theory, some of these reprofilings and restructurings could be

---

[20]Cumulative inflows into local currency bond markets from January 2020 to March 2022 were less than 0.5 percent of GDP, in contrast to the 2.8 percent of GDP and 1.9 percent of GDP seen in the runup to the 2013 taper tantrum and the 2015–16 Federal Reserve hiking cycle, respectively.

Figure 1.15. Frontier Market Access and Debt Vulnerabilities

Frontier market debt and debt servicing burdens have approximately doubled since 2010.

Market access has dropped sharply this year as financial conditions have tightened.

1. Frontier Debt-to-GDP and Interest-to-Revenue Ratios
(Percent, interquartile range)

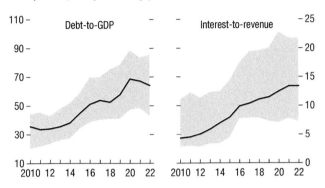

2. Frontier Market International Sovereign Hard Currency Issuance by Region
(Billions of US dollars)

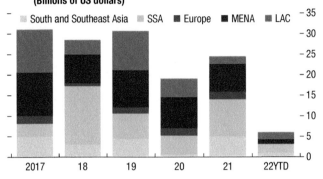

Frontier markets face significant bond maturities in 2023–25, which will be hard to roll over at current spreads.

External debt to private creditors accounts for more than one-third of external debt for many issuers that have traded at distressed levels this year.

3. Hard Currency Bond Maturities and Spreads
(Billions of US dollars)

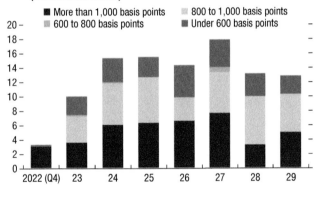

4. Public External Debt Composition by Spreads, 2020
(Percent)

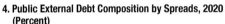

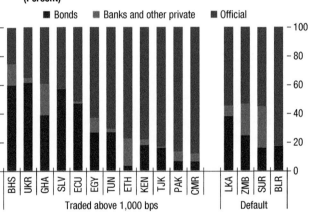

Sources: IMF, World Economic Outlook database; JPMorgan; World Bank, International Debt Statistics; and IMF staff calculations.
Note: In panel 4, data primarily refer to public and publicly guaranteed external debt from the World Bank international Debt Statistics where available, as of 2020, or World Bank Quarterly External Debt Statistics in instances where not available. Official debt is debt owed to bilateral and multilateral creditors. Zambia's external debt numbers comprise only foreign-currency-denominated debt. In August 2022, Ukraine's foreign creditors (for example, bondholders) backed its request for a two-year freeze (deferral) on debt service payments. Ukraine is not classified as a frontier market elsewhere. The grouping of >1,000 bps comprises those that have traded above 1,000 bps for an extended period at some point in 2022. In panel 4, data labels use International Organization for Standardization (ISO) country codes. bps = basis points; LAC = Latin America and the Caribbean; MENA = Middle East and North Africa; SSA = sub-Saharan Africa; YTD = year to date.

facilitated by the Group of Twenty (G20) Common Framework for eligible countries, but only three countries have requested to do so (Chad, Ethiopia, Zambia), and despite some progress no restructuring has yet been completed.[21]

---

[21]Sixty-nine low-income countries are eligible for the G20 Common Framework, for which an IMF-supported program is a precondition. Sri Lanka and Suriname are not.

In addition to the risks facing emerging and frontier economies with market access, a record number of low-income countries—most of which are largely dependent on official sector financing—are facing extremely precarious debt situations. These fragile countries, which already had limited fiscal and monetary policy room before the pandemic, have been weakened further by recent events. Current account deficits and reserves positions have generally worsened, though some have benefited from the commodity rally, and inflation has increased (in many cases due to exchange rate depreciation). According to the IMF's debt sustainability analyses, eight low-income countries are in debt distress and 30 are at high risk of distress (out of 69 countries considered low-income countries—among which, there are some frontier markets).[22] While the G20 Debt Service Suspension Initiative and other multilateral initiatives, such as the allocation of additional IMF special drawing rights to supplement member countries' official reserves, gave low-income countries temporary breathing room during the pandemic, debt service obligations have now resumed, and prospects for significant additional grants or concessional financing may fade.

China: Housing Risks Could Spread to the Banking Sector

The property sector downturn in China has deepened since the April 2022 GFSR because of a sharp decline in home sales during lockdowns that increased liquidity stress for property developers. In China, presale transactions—purchases of properties not yet built—have accounted for about 90 percent of total home sales in recent years, making presale receipts a major source of funding for developers (Figure 1.16, panel 1, black line). As access to market financing becomes increasingly difficult and presale receipts plummet, property developers face self-reinforcing liquidity pressure, which in turn diminishes their ability to complete ongoing construction. The recent call from home buyers to suspend mortgage payments for stalled presold properties has raised concern about the impact on financial institutions, putting downward pressure on equity prices of Chinese banks (Figure 1.16, panel 2). If unfinished housing is never completed and ends up in default, recovery values on these properties could be near zero, with significant negative implications for bank capital levels.

The acute liquidity stress raises concerns about broader solvency risks for developers. After building up leverage in recent years to raise turnover and expand inventories, a growing number of property developers have defaulted on their debt. These liquidity strains have been amplified by local governments' tighter

control over presale receipts in escrow accounts, in efforts to ensure the completion of presold properties. The continued decline in property prices has weighed on the value of inventories, amplifying developers' solvency pressure (Figure 1.16, panel 3). At prevailing market conditions, IMF staff analysis shows that 45 percent of property developers by assets might not be able to cover their debt obligations with earnings, and 20 percent of developers by assets could become insolvent if their inventory value is adjusted to current property prices. Delays in addressing the liquidity stress in the sector could further erode market confidence and suppress future earnings as well as access to credit. Offshore real estate bond prices have dropped sharply, suggesting that debt restructuring may be inevitable for a large share of the sector (Figure 1.16, panel 4). About 70 percent of offshore bonds trade at 40 cents on the dollar or less.

Property developer failures could spill over into the banking sector, affecting some vulnerable small banks and domestic systemically important banks in light of their lower capital buffers and higher property-related concentration risk. Local banks in certain areas—for example, where the stock of unfinished housing is large and local public finances are weak—could face sizable property-related credit losses. Overall, the banking sector's exposure to the property sector is large, with 8 percent of total lending to property developers and another 20 percent to mortgage borrowers.

IMF staff analysis shows that a shock resulting both from property developer defaults and home-buyer boycotts of mortgage payments would have a significant impact on bank balance sheets. Under a scenario in which 10 percent of the exposures to distressed property developers and 10 percent of the mortgage exposures related to unfinished properties become nonperforming loans with very low recovery values, 15 percent of banks in the sample, representing 10 percent of total banking system assets, would fail to meet minimum capital requirements.[23] The weak tail consists mostly of small banks and some domestic systemically important banks. Large banks, including all

---

[22]See https://www.imf.org/external/Pubs/ft/dsa/DSAlist.pdf.

[23]The assumption for distressed property developers is based on available disclosures by banks assessing their own credit risk. The extent of mortgages affected by the boycott or related to the troubled unfinished housing is unknown. The analysis is meant to gauge the downside risks to financial stability if mortgage suspension becomes more pervasive.

Figure 1.16. China: Property Sector

A key source of funding for property developers has dried up with the collapse in sales of presold homes during COVID-19 lockdowns.

1. Residential Real Estate Sales and Financing of Real Estate Investment
(Percent, year-over-year growth)

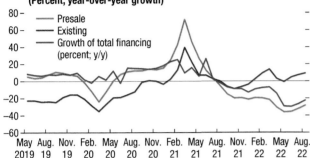

The recent homebuyers' mortgage payment boycott for presold properties has raised concerns about banks' profitability and resilience.

2. Bank Equity Performance
(Index, May 2021 = 100)

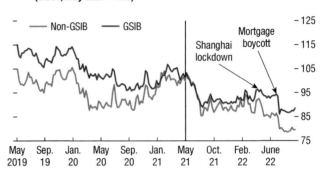

Some property developers lack sustainable debt-servicing capacity and/or face solvency risk.

3. Real Estate Firms: Share of Firms at Risk
(Percent of total risk-weighted assets)

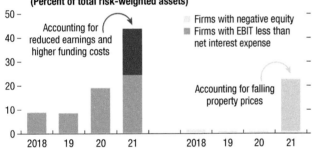

Many offshore bonds are being traded at distressed levels, suggesting that debt restructuring may be inevitable.

4. US Dollar Offshore Bond Prices
(Price index to end-2020)

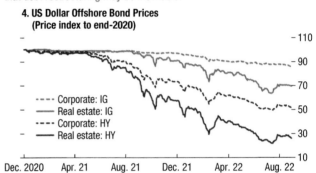

High defaults and low recoveries on presold property mortgages could significantly impair bank capital ...

5. Banks: Potential Credit Losses Related to Real Estate Exposure
(Percent of total risk-weighted assets)

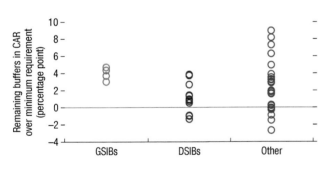

... and large stocks of unfinished houses may generate macro-financial spillovers in regions without fiscal space to contain risks.

6. Regional Public Debt and Housing Market Development
(Years; percent of GDP)

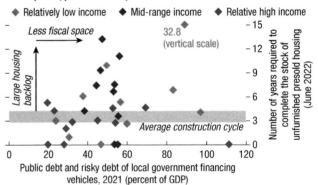

Sources: Bloomberg Finance L.P.; CEIC; S&P Capital IQ; and IMF staff calculations.
Note: In panel 3, the dark blue bar is based on a 20 percent drop in EBITDA and a 200 basis point increase in average funding costs; the dark yellow bar includes a 15 percent drop in inventory values. The analysis includes the following key assumptions: (1) 70 percent of net new mortgages each year are associated with presold houses; (2) 10 percent of unfinished presold houses fail to be delivered; and (3) loans to risky developers as a share of total real estate exposures are at 5 percent for GSIBs, 10 percent for DSIBs, and 15 percent for other banks. The minimum capital requirement is a 10.5 percent CAR for other banks, plus additional required buffers for DSIBs and GSIBs. In panel 6, presold unfinished houses are estimated based on cumulative home presales and housing construction since 2010. Risky debt of LGFVs is debt issued by LGFVs with EBIT lower than net interest expense for the past three years. CAR = capital adequacy ratio; DSIB = domestic systemically important bank; EBITDA = earnings before interest, taxes, depreciation, and amortization; GSIB = global systemically important bank; HY = high yield; IG = investment grade; LGFV = local government financing vehicle; y/y = year over year.

Figure 1.17. Market Liquidity Conditions

The standard market liquidity metrics show some signs of deterioration.

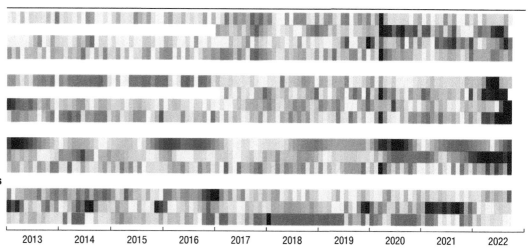

Equity markets
Bid-ask spread
Market depth
Turnover ratio
Return-to-volume ratio

Sovereign bond markets
Bid-ask spread
Market depth
Turnover ratio
Return-to-volume ratio

Corporate bond markets
Bid-ask spread
Turnover ratio
Return-to-volume ratio

Foreign exchange markets
Bid-ask spread
Trading volume
Return-to-volume ratio

2013 2014 2015 2016 2017 2018 2019 2020 2021 2022

Sources: Bloomberg Finance L.P.; Haver Analytics; Japan Bond Trading; JPMorgan Big Data and AI Strategies; MarketAxess; Reuters; Securities Industry and Financial Markets Association; and IMF staff calculations.
Note: Indicators are based on the maximum z-score among regions. Red (green) cells represent lowest (highest) liquidity levels. Regions are the euro area, Japan, and the United States for equity markets and Germany, Italy, Japan, the United Kingdom, and the United States for sovereign bond markets—except for market depth, which is for the United States. For equities and Japanese sovereign bonds, bid-ask spreads are estimated based on Corwin and Schultz (2012). For corporate bond markets, the bid-ask spread applies to the United States and the euro area, and other indicators apply to the United States. For sovereign bond markets, cash bond data are used for bid-ask spreads, and futures market data are used for the turnover ratio and return-to-volume ratio, except for the United States, which uses cash bond data. Market depth is the average amount of trading in futures expected to move the underlying market by 1 percent in a five-minute period. The turnover ratio captures trading frequency, calculated as trading volume divided by outstanding amounts of securities. The return-to-volume ratio reflects the sensitivity of price to the trading volume, which is calculated as the price change divided by trading volume.

global systemically important banks (GSIBs), appear to be resilient (Figure 1.16, panel 5).

With the economic slowdown and pandemic response constraining fiscal capacity, local governments are now saddled with ensuring the delivery of unfinished houses and handling distressed property developers amid falling revenues from land sales. With elevated debt levels and increased fiscal burdens, along with contingent liabilities arising from financially weak local government financing vehicles, this task may prove challenging. The stock of unfinished presold houses is sizable in a number of provinces with relatively low income and high public debt (Figure 1.16, panel 6). Should local government prove unable to support the real estate sector, there could be adverse spillovers to the broader corporate sector—where vulnerabilities are already high (see Box 1.1).[24]

[24]The authorities have announced several policies to support the real estate sector, including a property sector rescue fund authorized to raise up to RMB 300 billion, RMB 200 billion in special loans through policy banks, credit guarantees offered by China Bond Insurance Co. to support bond issuance by property developers, and a reduction in the five-year loan prime rate, with the minimum first-home mortgage rate set at 20 basis points below the five-year loan prime rate.

Poor Market Liquidity: A Shock Amplifier

After more than a decade of abundant liquidity and compressed volatility, the global move toward an aggressive tightening monetary cycle to fight high inflation—spanning several years—has substantially increased market volatility, especially in the rates space, contributing to a deterioration in market liquidity conditions.[25] Against a backdrop of heightened uncertainty about the economic and policy outlook, market liquidity metrics have worsened across asset classes, especially in the past few weeks amid deteriorating risk appetite. Bid-ask spreads have widened significantly, market depth has declined sharply, and liquidity premiums have increased (see Figure 1.17 and Figure 1.18, panel 1).

Deteriorating market liquidity conditions may pose risks to financial stability. The recent dramatic stress in the gilts market shows how sudden price moves

[25]Market liquidity refers to market participants' ability to buy and sell securities efficiently, without triggering large price changes. Note that *market liquidity* is not the same as the ample *monetary liquidity* injected into the financial system by central banks through large purchases of securities under quantitative easing programs.

Figure 1.18. Market Structure and Liquidity

The US Treasury bid-ask spread is elevated and market liquidity conditions have worsened.

1. US Treasury Bid-Ask Spread and Market Liquidity Index
(Basis points)

Markets need to keep absorbing sizable Treasury issuances as central banks reduce their purchases.

2. US Treasury Supply: Ten-Year-Equivalent Amount
(Billions of US dollars)

Foreign demand for US Treasuries could decrease as foreign exchange-hedged returns may become increasingly less attractive.

3. Excess Yield Spreads of Hedged US Treasury Yields over Local Government Bonds
(Basis points)

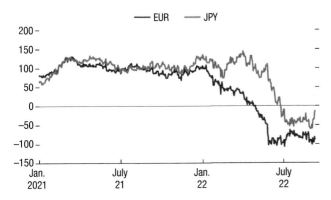

Banks appear less willing to deploy their balance sheets in a highly uncertain and volatile environment.

4. US Primary Dealer Positions and Overnight Indexed Swap (OIS) Implied Volatility
(Millions of US dollars, left scale; basis points, annualized, right scale)

The costs of international dollar short term funding have increased, reflecting precautionary demands amid a high level of uncertainty.

5. Cross Currency Basis Swap Against the US Dollar, 3 Month
(Basis points)

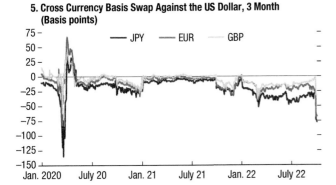

In the domestic dollar short-term funding market, the FRA-OIS spreads, a proxy of interbank credit risk, have been wider recently.

6. US Dollar FRA-OIS Spread
(Basis points, rolling 1st IMM date forwards)

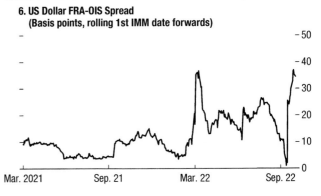

Sources: Bloomberg L.P.; Federal Reserve Bank of New York; JPMorgan Chase & Co.; TreasuryDirect; US Treasury; and IMF staff calculations.
Note: In panel 1, the market liquidity index is the average of Bloomberg US Government Securities Liquidity index and the JP Morgan US Treasury total root mean square error (RMSE) index. In panel 2, issuance excludes the Federal Reserve System Open Market Account (SOMA) absorption, and the Federal Reserve purchase excludes reinvestment. In panel 2, for the Treasury issuance projection, primary dealers' marketable borrowing estimates in the Treasury Borrowing Advisory Committee and securities outstanding data are used to estimate issuance amounts, and past auction data are used to project security and maturity composition. In panel 5, given the Libor transition and the discontinuity of benchmark indices since December 31, 2021, cross currency basis spreads are Libor-index-based before January 1, 2022, and OIS-based on and after the date. The data cutoff date for panels 5 and 6 is October 4, 2022. 2y2y = two-year, two-year; EUR = euro; Fed = Federal Reserve; JPY = Japanese yen; FRA-OIS = forward rate agreement-overnight index swap; IMM = international money market.

combined with forced selling and deleveraging dynamics can lead to disorderly conditions that could threaten broader market functioning and stability.

As central banks continue to tighten aggressively and remove liquidity (including by shrinking their balance sheets) and with market volatility rising across asset classes amid heightened uncertainty about the economic and policy outlook, investors have pulled back from risk taking in recent weeks. A more cautious investor posture implies larger cash and cash-equivalent holdings, driving more liquidity into US short-term funding markets.

In recent weeks, international short-term dollar funding markets have begun to show signs of concern amid an uncertain outlook. There has been a widening of the cross-currency basis swap spreads, a proxy for the marginal cost of offshore US dollar funding. The three-month cross-currency basis swaps (for the euro, and yen vs the US dollar) surged to their widest level since March 2020 (Figure 1.18, panel 5). Some seasonal technical factors—the three-month contract capturing the year-end when usually there is a higher demand for US dollars—combined with the global liquidity concerns have been at play. On the supply side, the increase in FRA-OIS spread (a measure of interbank credit risk, Figure 1.18, panel 6) and heightened currency volatility pose a risk of a potential drop in the supply of US dollar funding. On the demand side, the strengthening of the US dollar reduces the repayment capacity of (unhedged) borrowers outside the US, increasing their demand for synthetic US dollar funding. Markets seem concerned about further strains in the international short-term dollar funding market, which if persistent could trigger the activation of central bank international liquidity facilities, such as the Federal Reserve's swap lines, the Foreign and International Monetary Authorities Repo Facility, as well as existing IMF precautionary credit lines.

However, as central banks proceed with balance sheet normalization and investors continue to reprice risk, market liquidity conditions may deteriorate further. Monetary authorities in advanced economies have increased their footprint in sovereign bond markets as they have grown their balance sheets, contributing to the decline in liquidity premiums and funding costs.[26] All else equal, quantitative tightening implies

a reduction in central banks' demand for sovereign bonds, leaving more of these bonds in private hands, which could translate into a shallower pocket to absorb shocks and therefore higher liquidity premiums and lower market liquidity. Of course, liquidity conditions will also be a function of the future supply of government bonds, in terms of both volumes and maturity profiles, along with other factors, including risk management practices and the risk appetite of investors and financial institutions.

There is substantial uncertainty about how liquidity conditions will evolve as quantitative tightening continues. The supply of long-dated Treasuries is anticipated to remain large next year (Figure 1.18, panel 2), while foreign-exchange-hedged yields may become increasingly less attractive to foreign investors at a time of reduced demand by central banks (Figure 1.18, panel 3). In addition to these cyclical adjustments, a confluence of structural factors may contribute to further tightening of liquidity, especially during periods of stress. Such factors include more constrained dealer balance sheets, technological innovations, and a greater share of passive investors.

Significant shifts in market structure that have occurred since the global financial crisis may play a role in the provision of market liquidity. Regulatory reforms have led banks to reduce the capital allocated to the balance-sheet-intensive business of market making. As a result, liquidity seems to disappear at times, particularly during volatile market conditions (Figure 1.18, panel 4). Technological innovation facilitates a shift of market-making activities from bank dealers to nontraditional players, such as principal trading firms, potentially leading to more fragile market liquidity conditions. The largely algorithmic principal trading firms that are large players in the fixed-income interdealer market (where trading is typically accessible only by banks and large financial institutions) automatically pull back from markets when volatility increases sharply, potentially exacerbating illiquidity issues.

In addition, the rise of passive investing in recent years may also constrain market liquidity during stress episodes. For instance, the US S&P 500 index trackers and exchange-traded funds have more than doubled their assets, to an almost 20 percent share of the market in less than a decade. The growing role of passive investing that offers daily redemptions to retail investors, coupled with signs of increased herding and concentration, has made market liquidity more

[26]The research suggests that the presence of the central bank as a buyer in the market reduces liquidity premiums and lowers funding costs, contributing to improved market liquidity conditions (Christensen and Gillan 2022; Fernandez-Amador and others 2013).

vulnerable to rapid changes in sentiment.[27] Moreover, the ability of arbitrageurs such as hedge funds to take advantage of temporary price dislocations in asset markets, and therefore act as liquidity providers, may be limited. Restrictions in the leverage available from prime brokers—needed to conduct arbitrage trades such as cash-futures bond trades—and investor demands for tighter risk management and greater transparency may limit their ability to effectively conduct arbitrage.[28]

Corporate Sector: Is the Credit Cycle Turning?

The challenging macroeconomic and policy environment is putting pressure on the global corporate sector, with high-yield issuers the most vulnerable to a downturn. Although earnings in large publicly traded firms remain strong, higher labor and input costs are weighing on profitability. Corporate profit margins have started to contract from the highs supported by the economic reopening, with all major sectors (excluding energy) revising earnings forecasts downward (Figure 1.19, panel 1). Credit spreads have widened substantially across sectors, especially recently as investor appetite for risk has declined amid poor liquidity and elevated volatility (Figure 1.19, panel 2).[29] Spreads on sub-investment-grade credit such as high-yield bonds and leveraged loans have widened to a degree not seen since the spring of 2020. This has led to pullback in new issuance of risky debt, particularly high-yield bonds (Figure 1.19, panel 3). Almost half of lower-rated CCC credit is trading at distressed levels, and major credit rating agencies have revised their high-yield default outlooks and expect US defaults to rise in the next few months.

At small firms, bankruptcies have already started to increase this year in major advanced economies because such firms are more affected by rising borrowing costs and declining fiscal support, alongside higher labor and input costs that are difficult to pass

on to end consumers.[30] Going forward, a further rise in inflation and additional tightening by central banks could derail the recovery in the corporate sector coming out of the pandemic and put more debt at risk.

To explore these challenges, IMF staff members carried out a partial sensitivity analysis to estimate the increase in at-risk debt in response to a combined shock to revenues, cost of goods sold, and interest expense.[31] It centers on the interest coverage ratio, which captures how easily a firm can pay interest on its outstanding debt. The share of debt with an interest coverage ratio below 0 (indicating firms with negative profitability) rises quickly at all the types of firms, exceeding 50 percent at small firms, based on averages across advanced and emerging markets (Figure 1.19, panel 4).[32] The share of debt at firms with a low-to-moderate interest coverage ratio (between 0 and 3) increases to more than one-third at both large and midsize firms, especially among the group of emerging market economies.[33] This increase in debt-at-risk could result in losses at bank and nonbank financial institutions with significant exposures to highly indebted nonfinancial firms—a development that could amplify the shock.[34] Temporary and targeted government support may be needed to prevent the risk of a wave of bankruptcies at small firms and avoid spillovers to the financial system.

Leveraged Finance under Pressure

With investors aggressively pulling back from risk taking in recent weeks, conditions in leveraged finance have deteriorated materially, with spreads

---

[27]This rise of passive investing has also been associated with the overall increase in cross-asset correlations, which may indicate greater spillover risks across markets and, increasingly, systemic liquidity risk. See Chapter 1 of the April 2015 GFSR for further details.

[28]See Chapter 1 of the October 2014 GFSR.

[29]US investment-grade corporate bond spreads reportedly came under pressure at the end of September as a result of investors in the UK having to liquidate their positions to meet margin calls on leveraged positions in the gilt market.

[30]Small firms—as defined by the European Union and the United States—have assets of less than approximately $50 million. See Online Annex 1.1, Section B, in the April 2021 GFSR.

[31]The calibration of the sensitivity analysis is based on the two inflationary episodes in 1973–75 and 1978–82. Real retail sales, consumer prices, and producer prices are used as proxies for the volume, unit price, and unit cost of goods sold to generate shocks to firms' revenues and the cost of goods sold. The effective interest rate on debt is based on the increase in corporate bond yields during these episodes. For the calculation of the interest rate, large firms are assumed to have characteristics of investment-grade firms, small firms are assumed to have high-yield characteristics, and midsize firms are an average of investment grade and high yield.

[32]The interest coverage ratio is calculated as a firm's earnings before interest expense and taxes divided by interest expense for a given period.

[33]The countries included in the analysis are based on the corporate sector framework presented in the April 2021 GFSR: China, France, Germany, India, Italy, Japan, Mexico, Poland, Russia, Spain, Türkiye, the United Kingdom, and the United States.

[34]For more on private sector debt and the global recovery, see Chapter 2 in the April 2022 WEO.

Figure 1.19. Corporate Performance and Default Outlook

Profit margins have started to contract.

Corporate credit spreads have continued to widen since the April 2022 GFSR to reach about half the pandemic peaks ...

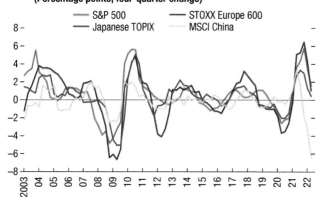

1. Corporate Profit Margins
   (Percentage points, four-quarter change)

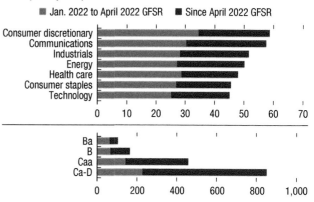

2. US Corporate Bond Spreads by Sector and Rating
   (Basis points)

... and new issuance has slowed as risky firms face tighter financial conditions.

Higher inflation and revenue decline would further worsen leverage metrics, especially at small firms.

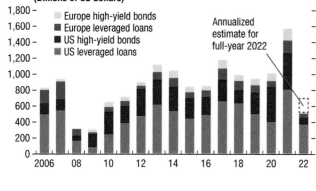

3. Issuance of US and European High-Yield Bonds and Leveraged Loans
   (Billions of US dollars)

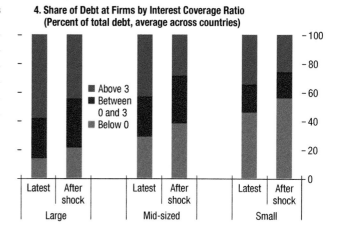

4. Share of Debt at Firms by Interest Coverage Ratio
   (Percent of total debt, average across countries)

Sources: Bloomberg L.P.; Haver Analytics; MSCI; PitchBook Leveraged Commentary and Data; Refinitiv Datastream IBES; S&P Capital IQ; and IMF staff calculations.
Note: In panel 2, "since April 2022 GFSR" refers to the period since April 18, 2022. In panel 4, interest coverage ratio is calculated by dividing a firm's earnings before interest and taxes by its interest expense during a given period. The analysis assumes the volume of goods sold declines by 7.5 percent, the price of the unit of goods sold increases by 13.4 percent, the cost of the unit of goods sold increases by 20.5 percent, and the effective interest rate on firms' total debt rises by 100 basis points for large firms, 312 basis points for medium firms, and 524 basis points for small firms. The country coverage is similar to that reported in the April 2021 *Global Financial Stability Report* (GFSR). In panel 4, large firms, medium firms, and small firms are defined as those having assets greater than $500 million, between $500 and $50 million, and less than $50 million, respectively.

widening sharply and issuance in the US leveraged loan market plunging in the third quarter to post-global-financial-crisis lows. Leveraged finance has historically been seen as a barometer of risk-taking in financial markets, and a worsening of conditions in this segment has historically been a harbinger of broader trends in investor risk appetite. Depending on (1) the funding structure of private lenders, (2) the horizon of investors, (3) the extent to which they may be holding concentrated positions, and (4) possible

linkages to the banking sector (for example, through lines of credit), a tightening of financial conditions could be amplified by the crystallization of balance sheet liquidity and credit risks embedded in this segment.

Against a challenging growth backdrop and elevated market volatility, some of the firms that have struggled to find financing in the high-yield bond and leveraged loan markets because of their small size, weaker liquidity position, or high debt levels are said to have

Figure 1.20. Developments in Leveraged Finance

Private credit has become a significant source of funding for risky firms.

1. Private Debt Assets under Management and US Leveraged Loans and High-Yield Bonds Outstanding
(Billions of US dollars)

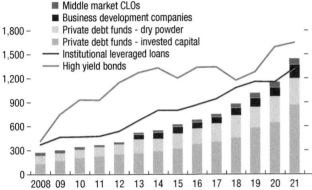

Credit quality is deteriorating, with the share of highly leveraged deals accelerating since the peak of the pandemic.

2. Leveraged Loan Issuance by Debt-to-EBITDA Ratio
(Percent)

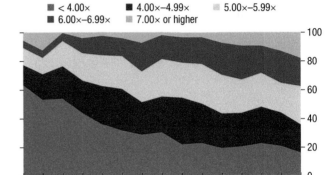

Asset managers and hedge funds remain the most exposed to riskier tranches of collateralized loan obligations (CLOs).

3. US CLO Investor Base
(Percent)

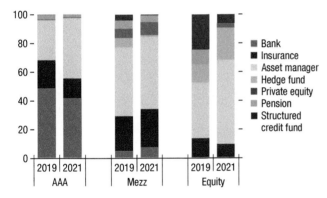

Private equity sponsors have played an increasing role in highly leveraged deals.

4. US Leveraged Buyout Transaction Volume by Type
(Percent of volume)

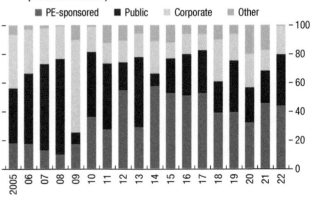

Sources: Citi; PitchBook Leveraged Commentary and Data; Preqin; S&P Global Ratings; UBS; and IMF staff calculations.
Note: CLO = collateralized loan obligation; Mezz = mezzanine; EBITDA = earnings before interest, taxes, depreciation and amortization; PE = private equity.

shifted to the more opaque and quickly expanding private credit market.[35] With lending standards tightening, the demand for private credit may continue to grow going forward. Taking a longer perspective, private credit has grown rapidly over the past decade or so, reaching $1.4 trillion at the end of 2021 and surpassing the size of the US institutional leveraged

loan market (Figure 1.20, panel 1). Owing in part to increased competition from private credit markets, leverage metrics on new loans in the leveraged loan market have hit new highs, with almost one-third of new loans having ratios of debt to earnings before interest, taxes, depreciation, and amortization greater than six times earnings (Figure 1.20, panel 2).

In the United States, lower-rated companies at higher risk of default make up an increasing share of leveraged finance, with more than 50 percent of the market now composed of firms with a B credit rating. The largest buyers of leveraged loans—collateralized loan obligations (CLOs)—have seen their average

---

[35]Private credit is provided by dedicated funds. It is often referred to as "direct lending" because it is not issued or traded in the public markets and the debt is not provided by the regulated bank market. Most private credit is provided as direct lending for private companies that cannot access or want to circumvent public markets, or that want certainty of execution and confidentiality.

holdings of B-rated loans more than double over the past five years. Concentration risks have also increased, with nearly 50 percent of the loan market composed of exposures to sectors such as technology, health care, and businesses services—all of which could face material margin pressures from higher input costs, including from inflation. Tighter financial conditions, mounting liquidity strains, and decelerating earnings growth could presage ratings downgrades and eventual defaults. An increase in the share of assets rated CCC or below could result in lower returns for equity and lower-rated CLO investors.[36] The underperformance of these investors could lead to a decline in new CLO issuance and a credit crunch in the leveraged loan market, reducing funding available to existing sub-investment-grade firms. By contrast, banking sector exposures in the CLO market are mostly concentrated in senior AAA tranches and thus are less likely to face credit losses (Figure 1.20, panel 3).

Private equity sponsors have also looked to private credit lenders to provide debt financing to the companies they buy, particularly in more risky leveraged buyout transactions (Figure 1.20, panel 4). Boosted by unprecedented policy support measures during the pandemic aimed at reopening capital markets and supporting the flow of credit to households and firms, leveraged buyout activity has boomed, with deal size increasing and valuations reaching record highs.[37] Highly leveraged and richly priced transactions have supported both private equity portfolio growth and private credit lending opportunities. In 2022 to date, leveraged buyout volumes have slowed considerably and are down 30 percent from 2021 as weaker risk sentiment has put a lid on new issuance. The credit quality of some of these assets may be tested during a recession. However, because most of this private lending remains very opaque, it may be hard for investors and regulators to assess credit risk until the credit cycle has already turned.

Housing Markets: At a Tipping Point?

Since the onset of the pandemic, house prices have surged by more than 20 percent in some economies (Figure 1.21, panel 1). A range of factors, some specific

to the pandemic, have contributed to these large price gains. Economic activity has recovered much faster than originally expected, with unprecedented fiscal and monetary policy measures helping maintain low debt service ratios. Supply bottlenecks have led to shrinking inventories, boosting house prices. As a result, the price-to-income ratio has reached its highest level in the past two decades in many countries, pointing to a deterioration in housing affordability (Figure 1.21, panel 2).[38]

As central banks around the globe aggressively tighten monetary policy to tackle price pressures, soaring borrowing costs and tighter lending standards, coupled with stretched house valuations, could lead to a sharp decline in house prices, especially in countries with a higher share of variable-rate mortgage debt. The pass-through of monetary policy tightening and higher interest rates to residential mortgage markets has already been swift in the United States, with the average fixed-rate 30-year mortgage hitting highs last seen in 2008, before declining somewhat in midyear 2022.[39] In some countries, global growth in real house prices had already moderated at the end of 2021, with substantial differences across and within regions (Figure 1.21, panel 1). For example, real house price growth was about 11 percent (year over year) in central and eastern Europe in the fourth quarter of 2021, while it was considerably lower in emerging Asia, Latin America, and the Middle East and North Africa regions.

In a severely adverse scenario, real house price declines over the next three years could be nearly 25 percent in emerging markets (Figure 1.21, panel 3). In advanced economies, real house prices could fall more than 10 percent in such a scenario. In this context, as shown in Figure 1.21, panel 4, affordability pressures (yellow bars) and deteriorating economic prospects (green bars) are key drivers of downside risk to house prices across most regions. Compared to the estimates in the October 2021 GFSR, in a downside

---

[36]For more on risky credit markets, see Chapter 2 in the April 2020 GFSR.

[37]Valuations of some firms have been reportedly inflated by circular deals involving private equity sponsors. See Wiggins (2022).

[38]The price-to-income ratio is calculated as the nominal house price index divided by nominal disposable income.

[39]Rapidly rising policy and mortgage rates, together with the cessation of purchases of mortgage-backed securities (MBSs) by the Federal Reserve since March 2022 (excluding reinvestments), have been accompanied by a sharp drop in refinancing rates since the spring, which has led to a significant decline in MBS repayment rates and a notable widening in MBS spreads. This suggests that, barring sales, MBS holdings will likely continue to be a substantial part of the Federal Reserve System Open Market Account portfolio in the medium term.

Figure 1.21. Housing Sector Trends

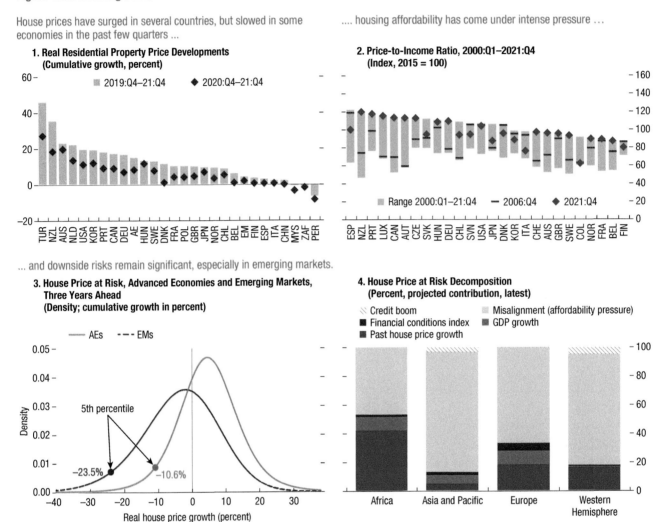

House prices have surged in several countries, but slowed in some economies in the past few quarters ...

1. Real Residential Property Price Developments
(Cumulative growth, percent)

.... housing affordability has come under intense pressure ...

2. Price-to-Income Ratio, 2000:Q1–2021:Q4
(Index, 2015 = 100)

... and downside risks remain significant, especially in emerging markets.

3. House Price at Risk, Advanced Economies and Emerging Markets, Three Years Ahead
(Density; cumulative growth in percent)

4. House Price at Risk Decomposition
(Percent, projected contribution, latest)

Sources: Bank for International Settlements; Bloomberg L.P.; Haver Analytics; IMF, World Economic Outlook database; Organisation for Economic Co-operation and Development; and IMF staff calculations.
Note: In panel 1, nominal house prices are adjusted for inflation using the consumer price index. Panels 3 and 4 show the estimation results from a house-prices-at-risk model. The model allows prediction of house price growth in a severely adverse scenario; that is, the range of outcomes in the lower tail of the future house price distribution. Probability densities are estimated for the three-year-ahead (cumulative) house price growth distribution across advanced economies and emerging markets. Filled circles indicate the price decline in the severely adverse scenario with a 5 percent probability (5th percentile). Panel 4 shows the projected contribution of the key drivers of house-price-at-risk projections in percent and by country area. Misalignment refers to the deviation of house-price-to-GDP per capita from an estimated trend and is used as a simple measure of the deviation of house prices from fundamentals (that is, overvaluation). In panels 1 and 2, data labels use International Organization for Standardization (ISO) country codes. AEs = advanced economies; EMs = emerging markets.

scenario the current projections imply a 2 percentage point larger price decline for emerging markets and a 3 percentage point smaller decline for advanced economies.[40]

[40]In comparison, median real house price growth is estimated to be about 5 percent over the next three years in some regions. The findings imply that the global house price boom will slow in a scenario with a 50 percent probability. For the housing-at-risk methodology, see Chapter 2 of the April 2019 GFSR.

Such risks could be greater in a scenario in which there is a sharp tightening of global financial conditions, which could increase the probability of a recession in the next few years. Although the severity and the macroeconomic implications of a shock originating in the housing market will depend crucially on the extent of house price correction and the distribution of household debt, some key mitigating factors are the stronger capital position of banks and more conservative loan underwriting standards since the global financial crisis. As a result, the potential contagion effect through the banking sector in the event of a large house price correction is likely to be more limited than in previous recessions. That said, risks may be emerging elsewhere in the housing sector, especially in the United States, where the nonbank financial institution sector has started to play a larger role in the securitized mortgage market.[41]

Global Banks: Stagflation Would Challenge the Resilience of the Banking Sector

The banking system has been resilient throughout the pandemic and the war in Ukraine, with high levels of capital and ample liquidity buffers. The global common equity Tier 1 (CET1) ratio increased from 12.5 percent in 2019 to 14.1 percent in 2021.[42] Banks' interest income has improved, benefiting from monetary policy normalization and rising rates. At large dealer banks, profits have also been boosted by trading income amid high market volatility. Balance sheet growth has continued. The asset mix shifted toward liquid assets and securities during the pandemic as deposits rose due to government support programs. Starting in 2021, loan growth has rebounded, and it is at pre-pandemic levels.[43] Liquidity and funding conditions remain healthy, with cash and reserves still above pre-pandemic levels.

With risks to the economic outlook squarely tilted to the downside, banks are rebuilding their loan-loss reserves for the first time since the pandemic. Lending conditions have tightened notably in recent quarters, with lending standards for corporate credit becoming more restrictive (Figure 1.22, panel 1). At the same time, demand for credit remains robust in advanced economies, reflecting firms' need for working capital because of higher input prices and ongoing supply chain disruptions. Meanwhile, credit demand has started to slow in emerging markets. A growing number of lending officers have expressed diminishing risk tolerance on concerns about the economic outlook and borrower credit risk, particularly in the euro area (Figure 1.22, panel 2). To evaluate the challenges facing the banking sector in the event of a crystallization of risks to the growth and inflation outlook, IMF staff members carried out a Global Bank Stress Test to assess the resilience of the banking sector in the event of a severe stagflation scenario.

The Global Bank Stress Test assumes a pandemic resurgence and continuation of geopolitical tensions that result in persistent disruptions in the global supply chain, including disruption in Russian gas exports to Europe. The scenario calibrates a de-anchoring of inflation expectations and a disorderly tightening of financial conditions, with spillovers through real and financial shocks across economies, which send the global economy into recession in 2023.[44] (The baseline scenario corresponds to the October 2022 WEO [Figure 1.23].)

In aggregate, the global banking system has sufficient capital to absorb losses under the stress scenario, benefiting from the reforms since the global financial crisis and the buildup of capital over the past years. In the stress scenario, the global CET1 ratio declines from 14.1 percent in 2021 to a minimum of 11.4 percent in 2023, barely recovering to 11.5 percent in 2024 (Figure 1.24, panel 1). The positive contributions to the CET1 ratio from higher interest income on performing loans are offset by the negative contributions from higher loan impairments and larger other expenses.

In the stress scenario, emerging market banks face greater losses than advanced economy banks. The maximum drop in the CET1 ratio, from 2021, reaches 4.3 percentage points for emerging market banks, 1.7 percentage points larger than for advanced economy banks (Figure 1.24, panel 1). By the end of 2024, the CET1 ratio for emerging market banks

---

[41]House price corrections can also have broader economic implications by affecting the residential component of fixed capital formation as well as the expected effective returns for property developers. For a discussion of risks that could also emerge from the exposure of nonbanks to the housing sector, see the October 2021 GFSR.

[42]Tier 1 capital is the core measure of a bank's financial strength from a regulator's point of view. CET1 is a component of Tier 1 capital. It encompasses ordinary shares and retained earnings.

[43]During the 2015–18 tightening cycle, banks ran down their cash balances and other securities while increasing lending and holdings of Treasury securities. This year, the growth in loans has been accompanied by a reduction in cash balances from high levels. So far, there is little evidence of banks shedding Treasuries or reducing their securities portfolios more generally.

[44]The IMF Global Bank Stress Test examined 262 banks from 28 countries accounting for 70 percent of global sector assets. The 28 countries in the sample are Australia, Austria, Belgium, Brazil, Canada, Denmark, Finland, France, Germany, Greece, India, Indonesia, Ireland, Italy, Japan, the Republic of Korea, Mexico, The Netherlands, Norway, Portugal, Saudi Arabia, South Africa, Spain, Sweden, Switzerland, Türkiye, the United Kingdom, and the United States.

Figure 1.22. Tightening Bank Lending Standards

Lending standards have tightened notably as credit demand continues to rise ...

... due to uncertainties around the economic outlook and borrower credit risk.

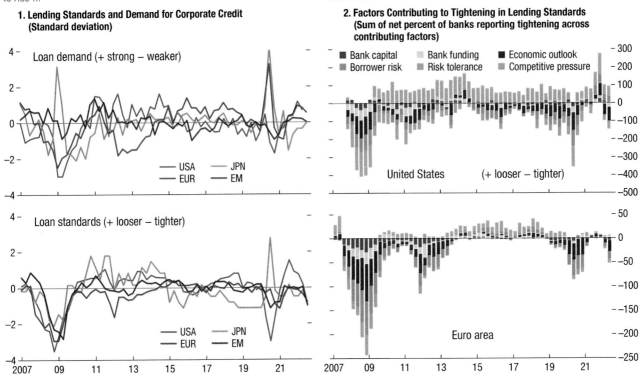

1. Lending Standards and Demand for Corporate Credit
(Standard deviation)

2. Factors Contributing to Tightening in Lending Standards
(Sum of net percent of banks reporting tightening across contributing factors)

Sources: National central banks; and IMF staff calculations.
Note: EM = emerging market; EUR = euro area; JPN = Japan; USA = United States.

Figure 1.23. Macro-Financial Scenario: Baseline and Stress Scenarios

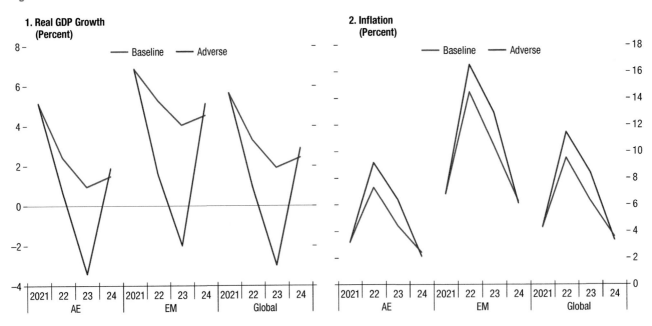

1. Real GDP Growth
(Percent)

2. Inflation
(Percent)

Sources: IMF, World Economic Outlook (WEO) database; and IMF staff calculations.
Note: Calibration of the scenario is based on the Global Macrofinancial Model (Vitek 2018). The adverse stress scenario is considerably more severe than the October 2022 WEO downside scenario. AE = advanced economy; EM = emerging market.

Figure 1.24. Impact on Global Banks of a Stress Scenario

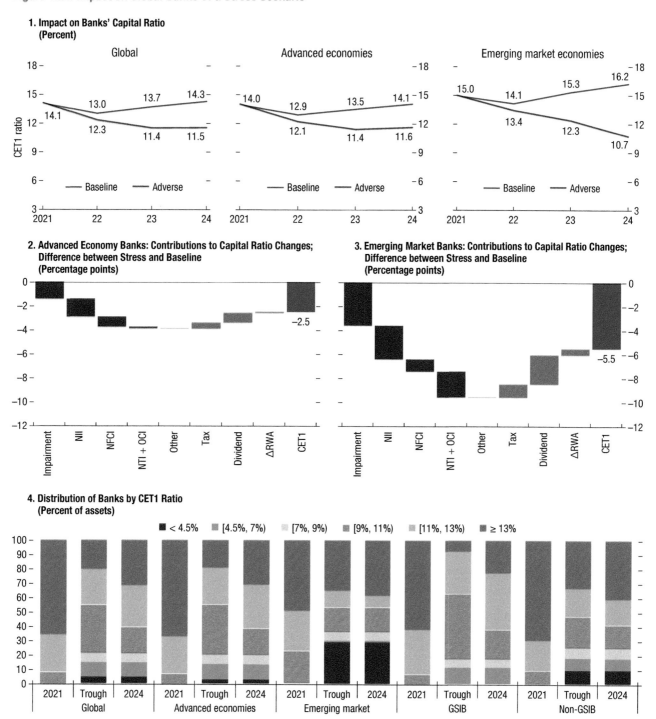

1. Impact on Banks' Capital Ratio
(Percent)

2. Advanced Economy Banks: Contributions to Capital Ratio Changes; Difference between Stress and Baseline
(Percentage points)

3. Emerging Market Banks: Contributions to Capital Ratio Changes; Difference between Stress and Baseline
(Percentage points)

4. Distribution of Banks by CET1 Ratio
(Percent of assets)

Sources: Fitch Connect; and IMF staff estimates.
Note: In panels 2 and 3, all contributions pertain to the weighted average global sample of 262 underlying banks from 28 countries. The panel presents the differences of the contributions under the stress and baseline scenarios. "Impairment" refers to loan losses. "Other" denotes the residual of the pretax income and expense flows that are not otherwise listed separately; that is, covering other operating income and expenses, where administrative expense is a sizable component. CET1 = common equity Tier 1; GSIB = global systemically important bank; NFCI = net fee and commission income; NII = net interest income; NTI = net trading income; OCI = other comprehensive income; RWA = risk-weighted assets.

under the stress scenario stands 5.5 percentage points below the baseline, compared to 2.5 percentage points for advanced economy banks.

The larger stress losses for emerging markets relative to advanced economy banks stem from their greater sensitivity to macrofinancial shocks. This translates into higher loan impairment, larger declines in net interest income, higher mark-to-market losses on their trading books ("NTI + OCI" components), and higher other expenses (Figure 1.24, panels 2 and 3). The larger trading losses are due to sharper increases in short-term interest rates and a higher share of government securities in their portfolios. The impact on emerging market banks is also more severe because some of them face additional financial vulnerabilities arising from a high share of debt denominated in foreign currency in their corporate or sovereign sectors.

While no country banking system would fail to meet the minimum 4.5 percent CET1 ratio under the stress scenario, several individual institutions would fall below that threshold. These more distressed cases account for 5 percent of total global assets in the sample and would require $77 billion to bring the CET1 ratio back to 4.5 percent (Figure 1.24, panel 4). The majority of these cases are emerging market banks, representing 29 percent of emerging market bank assets in the sample. Among GSIBs, no bank would fall below the minimum 4.5 percent threshold, although 11 percent of GSIBs (by bank assets) would need to dip into their capital conservation buffers (CCBs).[45] With respect to non-GSIBs, banks accounting for 10 percent of total assets would fail to meet the 4.5 percent minimum threshold. To rebuild the CCB and GSIB buffers, as well as the capital shortfall below the 4.5 percent minimum CET1 ratio, the overall capital need would amount to about $214 billion.[46]

Policy Recommendations

With inflation climbing to highs not seen in decades and price pressures broadening beyond food and energy prices, policymakers around the world

have continued to normalize monetary policy. The pace of tightening is accelerating in many countries, particularly in advanced economies, in terms of both the frequency and the magnitude of rate hikes. Some central banks have begun to reduce the size of their balance sheets, moving further toward normalization. A tightening in financial conditions is necessary to restore price stability. While it cannot resolve remaining pandemic-related bottlenecks in global supply chains and disruptions in commodity markets due to the war in Ukraine, monetary policy can slow domestic demand to address widespread demand-related inflationary pressures.[47]

Price stability is a crucial prerequisite for sustained and inclusive economic growth. With risks to the inflation outlook tilted to the upside, central banks should continue to normalize policy to prevent inflationary pressures from becoming entrenched. They need to act resolutely to bring inflation back to target, avoiding any de-anchoring of inflation expectations that would damage credibility built over the past several decades. Policymakers should heed the lessons of the past: moving too slowly to restrain inflation and restore price stability requires a more costly subsequent tightening and entails more painful and disruptive economic adjustments later. The historical experience of the US monetary policy in the 1970s and early 1980s offers clear lessons. It is important for central banks to keep this experience in their sights as they navigate the difficult road ahead.

With policy rates moving away from the effective lower bound that has prevailed in many countries since the global financial crisis, policymakers should rethink the modalities and objectives of the forward guidance they provide.[48] The high uncertainty clouding the economic and inflation outlook hampers the ability of central banks to provide explicit and precise guidance about the future path of monetary policy. But clear communication about their policy function—objectives, intertemporal trade-offs, and steps required to bring inflation down to target— and their unwavering commitment to achieve their

---

[45]The CCB is used to absorb losses in times of stress. In such instances, regulators would need to remain ready to communicate to banks that capital buffers may be used (see Abad and Garcia Pascual 2022).

[46]Compared to the previous Global Bank Stress Test in October 2020 GFSR, the share of banks with capital shortfall is similar, either against the barebone minimum 4.5 percent CET1 ratio or the broader threshold that includes CCB and GSIB buffers. However, the dollar amount of capital shortfall is smaller thanks to higher capital base at the beginning of the stress test horizon.

[47]For a discussion of main supply and demand drivers of inflation, as well as forecast errors, see Chapter 1 of the October 2022 WEO and Box 1.1.

[48]Forward guidance about the future path of policy rates is particularly useful at the effective lower bound of nominal interest rates as it helps reduce longer-term interest rates by guiding lower expected short-term interest rates.

mandated objectives is crucial to preserve credibility. Clear communication about the need to further normalize policy in line with the evolving inflation outlook is also essential to ensure orderly market reaction and avoid unwarranted volatility. There is a risk that financial conditions may tighten sharply and economic growth slow more than anticipated in coming months, prompting calls for a pause in policy normalization. Authorities should be wary of such calls and consider deploying appropriate tools in case of market dysfunction. It is critical to avoid a stop-go policy normalization path that could undermine price stability and result in a disorderly tightening of financial conditions—a tightening that, by inter-acting with existing financial vulnerabilities, could put economic growth and financial stability at risk down the road.

Monetary policy can get support from tighter fiscal policy in achieving the mandated inflation objective (see the October 2022 *Fiscal Monitor*). In addition, to help limit governments' debt burden, fiscal consolidation would ease aggregate demand pressure on prices, moderating the extent of policy normalization required to rein in inflation. Within budget constraints, governments can reprioritize spending to protect the most vulnerable from the sharp rise in food and energy prices.

The euro area faces a particularly challenging environment, with differences across member states in terms of inflation, economic prospects, and funding needs. Against this backdrop, it is essential to be able to deploy appropriate tools to ensure that the mon-etary policy stance is transmitted smoothly across all euro area countries while countering unwarranted, dis-orderly market dynamics. The recent announcement of the Transmission Protection Instrument is a welcome step to address fragmentation risks.

Emerging and frontier markets remain vulnerable to a sharp tightening in global financial conditions and capital outflows. While there is still significant variation across countries in terms of the economic and inflation outlook, as well as in policy responses, central banks have generally continued to tighten monetary policy to address inflationary pressures. Rate increases should proceed as warranted based on country-specific circumstances to preserve policy credibility and anchor inflation expectations. Countries with highly vulner-able financial sectors, limited or no fiscal space, and significant external financing needs are already under

strong pressure and could face further severe challenges in the event of a disorderly tightening of conditions. Countries with credible medium-term fiscal plans, clearer policy frameworks, and stronger financing arrangements will be better positioned to manage such tightening. There is a need to rebuild fiscal space and buffers.

The IMF's Integrated Policy Framework provides a useful architecture for emerging market economies to actively manage the risks stemming from the global tightening cycle and the stronger US dollar. Depending on exchange rate flexibility, foreign exchange market depth, the level of foreign exchange mismatches, and the degree of anchoring of inflation expectations, different actions may be called for. In light of contin-ued volatility in financial markets, the use of foreign exchange interventions may be appropriate in the presence of frictions, so long as reserves are sufficient and intervention does not impair the credibility of macroeconomic policies or substitute for their neces-sary adjustment. In case of crises or imminent crises, capital flow management measures may be an option for some countries to lessen outflow pressures. Any outflow capital flow management measures introduced during such cases should be part of a comprehensive policy package that tackles underlying macroeconomic imbalances, and lifted once crisis conditions abate.

Sovereign borrowers in developing economies and frontier markets should enhance efforts to contain risks associated with their high debt vulnerabilities, includ-ing through early contact with their creditors, multi-lateral cooperation, and support from the international community. Continued use of enhanced collective action clauses in international sovereign bonds and the development of majority voting provisions in syndicated loans would help facilitate future debt restructurings. For countries near debt distress, bilateral and private sector creditors should find ways to coordi-nate on preemptive restructuring to avoid costly hard defaults and prolonged loss of market access. Where applicable, the G20 Common Framework should be utilized. Value recovery instruments, such as GDP—or commodity—linked warrants, could play an import-ant role in improving the outcomes of restructurings during this period of high economic uncertainty. Countries with moderate risk of debt distress but with elevated liquidity risks should consider liability management operations through debt exchanges or refinancing operations.

Policymakers should promote the depth of local currency markets in emerging markets and foster a stable and diversified investor base. Local currency markets continue to be a key funding channel for emerging markets. Measures should strive to (1) establish a sound legal and regulatory framework for securities, (2) develop efficient money markets, (3) enhance transparency of both primary and secondary markets as well as the predictability of issuance, (4) bolster market liquidity, and (5) develop a robust market infrastructure.

Policymakers should continue to contain a further buildup of financial vulnerabilities. While considering country-specific circumstances and the near-term economic challenges, they should adjust selected macroprudential tools as needed to tackle pockets of elevated vulnerabilities while avoiding a disorderly tightening of financial conditions. If such tools are not available—for example, in the nonbank financial institution sector—policymakers should urgently develop them. Striking a balance between containing the buildup of vulnerabilities and avoiding procyclicality and a disorderly tightening of financial conditions is important in light of heightened uncertainty about the economic outlook, the ongoing policy normalization process, and the limited fiscal space remaining after the pandemic.

Developments and risks in global housing markets during the ongoing cycle of monetary tightening should be carefully monitored. National authorities should deploy stringent stress tests to estimate the potential impact of a sharp fall in house prices on household balance sheets and ultimately on financial institutions. On the macroprudential policy front, policymakers who had previously tightened macroprudential tools (such as stressed debt-service and loan-to-value ratios) to address overheating conditions in the housing sector should consider whether there is a need to revisit that decision to prevent severe macroeconomic implications in the event of sharp repricing in housing markets.

In China, further action led by the central government is urgently needed to restore stability in the housing market. A more robust and effective response should entail credible policy mechanisms at minimum taxpayer cost to ensure the completion of presold housing, restructure distressed developers, and restore home buyer confidence. Contingency planning to safeguard financial stability should be prepared, along with macroeconomic policy support and medium-term structural reforms needed to secure an orderly transition to a sustainable financial model for property developers.

The results of the Global Bank Stress Test suggest that the global banking system would remain resilient in a severe stagflation scenario. However, some advanced economy banks and 29 percent of the largest emerging market banks (by assets) would need additional capital. Against a worsening economic outlook, authorities should ensure that bank asset classifications and loan-loss provisions accurately reflect credit risk and losses. Supervisors should ensure that banks have risk management systems commensurate with their risk profile, including strengthening the capacity and adequacy of stress tests. Adequate capital buffers are essential to containing financial stability risks. Financial institutions should have adequate capital conservation plans, and any significant decline in capital ratios should be accompanied by a credible plan to restore capital.

To ensure comprehensive and timely assessment of risks in credit markets, authorities should ensure that they have sufficient and reliable data to analyze vulnerabilities stemming from origination practices and chains of intermediation in the corporate debt market. Transparency in the growing private debt market should be enhanced, including through collection of data on cross-border exposures. Given the increasingly prominent role of nonbank financial institutions in intermediating global credit, ensuring adequate risk management practices in nonbank financial institutions and their horizon scanning and supervision by prudential authorities are vital. To deal with private debt overhang, restructuring and insolvency tools should help ensure efficient and orderly exit of nonviable firms facing structural challenges (see the October 2020 GFSR and Chapter 2 of the April 2022 WEO). However, some firms and sectors facing credit constraints may still need short-term fiscal support. Such support should continue to depend on firms' viability and available fiscal space and be limited to circumstances in which there was clear market access failure.

Swift implementation of policies to mitigate market liquidity risks is paramount to avoid possible amplification of shocks, especially during the ongoing normalization of monetary policy. Supervisory authorities should monitor the robustness of trading infrastructures and support transparency in markets. In addition, improving the availability of data at the trade level would help the private and public sectors with timely assessment of liquidity risks in markets. Given the increasing importance of nonbank financial institutions such as principal trading firms and hedge funds in the provision of liquidity in key funding markets, counterparties should carefully monitor intraday activity and leverage exposures, strengthen their liquidity risk management practices, and enhance transparency and data availability.

The correction in crypto asset markets has added extra urgency to the call for comprehensive and consistent regulation and adequate supervision. Policymakers need to address risks to users and investors, to market and financial integrity, and to macro-financial stability. The regulatory framework should cover all critical activities and entities. Crypto asset service providers that deliver core functions and generate key risks should be licensed, registered, or authorized. These include entities related to the storage, transfer, exchange, and custody of reserves—among others—which should be subject to regulation similar to that of financial service providers (following the principle of "same activity, same risk, same regulation"). Strong international cooperation is essential to provide guidance, ensure consistent implementation, and contain spillover risks.

Box 1.1. Indicator-Based Framework Update

Amid the rise in inflation globally, and associated actions to tighten monetary policy, several sectors across advanced economies and emerging markets continue to look vulnerable in an environment of

tightening financial conditions.[1] Financial vulnerabilities have increased across emerging market sectors and remain elevated in advanced economy sovereign and nonbank financial sectors.

The authors of this box are Yingyuan Chen, Fabio Cortes, Deepali Gautam, Frank Hespeler, Thomas Piontek, and Aki Yokoyama.

[1]The focus of the framework is restricted to on-balance-sheet vulnerabilities, given the absence of available data for off-balance-sheet vulnerabilities for a cross-section of countries. Due to the nature of the data and their reporting frequency, most of the current data points are through the fourth quarter of 2021.

Figure 1.1.1. Global Financial Vulnerabilities

1. Proportion of Economies with Elevated Vulnerabilities, by Sector
(Percent of countries with high and medium-high vulnerabilities, by GDP [assets of banks, asset managers, other financial institutions, and insurers]; number of vulnerable countries in parentheses)

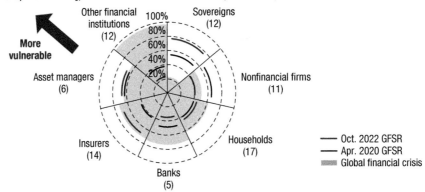

2. Financial Vulnerabilities by Sector and Region

	Sovereigns		Nonfinancial Firms		Households		Banks		Insurers		Asset Managers		Other Financial Institutions	
	Apr. 2020	Oct. 2022	Apr. 2020	Oct. 2022	Apr. 2020	Oct. 2022	Apr. 2020	Oct. 2022	Apr. 2020	Oct. 2022	Apr. 2020	Oct. 2022	Apr. 2020	Oct. 2022
Advanced Economies														
United States														
Euro area														
Other advanced														
Emerging Market Economies														
China														
Other emerging														

Sources: Banco de Mexico; Bank for International Settlements; Bank of Japan; Bloomberg Finance L.P.; China Insurance Regulatory Commission; European Central Bank; Haver Analytics; IMF, Financial Soundness Indicators database; IMF, World Economic Outlook (WEO) database; Reserve Bank of India; S&P Global Market Intelligence; S&P Leveraged Commentary and Data; Securities and Exchange Commission of Brazil; Securities and Exchange Board of India; WIND Information Co.; and IMF staff calculations.
Note: See technical annex of the April 2019 *Global Financial Stability Report* (GFSR) for details on the Indicator-Based Framework. In panel 1, "global financial crisis" shows the maximum vulnerability value during 2007–08. In panel 2, dark red shading indicates a value in the top 20 percent of pooled samples (advanced and emerging market economies pooled separately) for each sector during 2000–22 (or longest sample available), and dark green shading indicates values in the bottom 20 percent. For the sovereign sector, the April 2020 data were adjusted to use updated pre-COVID data where WEO forecasts were previously employed. Other advanced economies comprise Australia, Canada, Denmark, Hong Kong Special Administrative Region, Japan, Korea, Norway, Singapore, Sweden, Switzerland, and the United Kingdom. Other emerging market economies are Brazil, India, Mexico, Poland, Russia, and Türkiye.

Box 1.2. The European Central Bank's New Tool to Contain Fragmentation Risk: The Transmission Protection Instrument

With the European Central Bank (ECB) proceeding to normalize monetary policy, fragmentation risk has come back into focus in markets—a development reminiscent of investor concerns during the euro area sovereign debt crisis in early 2010s. While the ECB has been engaged in a hiking cycle to bring inflation back to target, the Transmission Protection Instrument, announced in July 2022, is intended to address the fragmentation risk that could impair the effective transmission of monetary policy across the euro area countries (ECB 2022).

As stated by the ECB, the first line of defense against risks to the transmission mechanism related to the COVID-19 pandemic is the reinvestment flexibility of purchases of maturing assets under the Pandemic Emergency Purchase Programme (PEPP). While the ability to skew asset purchases toward

the debt of certain euro area countries allows for the use of redemptions to address these risks, PEPP reinvestments are anticipated to continue only until 2024. This limits its use as a long-term tool to ensure the efficient transmission of monetary policy, also because any deviation from the capital key rule will eventually have to be reversed at some point. Moreover, while PEPP's projected monthly reinvestments are sizeable, they appear to be smaller than the expected gross sovereign debt issuance—to address fragmentation risk (Figure 1.2.1, panel 1). Thus, with net asset purchases having come to an end in the first half of 2022, the fiscal deficit in the euro area is, for the first time in several years, set to exceed ECB reinvestments going forward (Figure 1.2.1, panel 2). Since the tapering of asset purchases was first announced in September 2021,

Figure 1.2.1. Fragmentation Risk in the Euro Area

Flexible reinvestments by the Pandemic Emergency Purchase Programme (PEPP) are unlikely to fully offset gross sovereign debt issuance by southern European countries.

The European Central Bank is stepping down as a significant buyer of euro area sovereign debt in both its Asset Purchase Programme and Pandemic Emergency Purchase Programme.

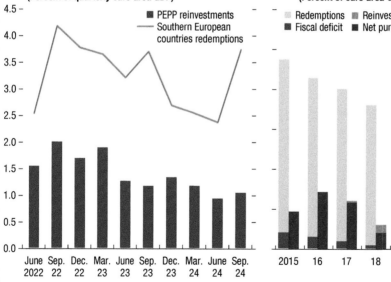

1. Projected Monthly PEPP Reinvestments and Sovereign Debt Redemptions until December 2024
(Percent of quarterly euro area GDP)

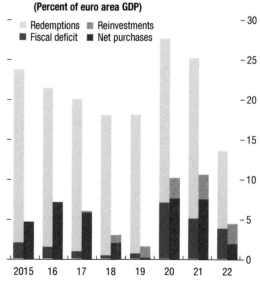

2. Euro Area: Budget Deficit and Sovereign Debt Purchases
(Percent of euro area GDP)

Sources: Bloomberg L.P.; European Central Bank; and IMF staff calculations.
Note: Southern European countries comprise Greece, Italy, Portugal, and Spain. PEPP = pandemic emergency purchase programme.

The authors of this box are Esti Kemp and Johannes Kramer.

Box 1.2 *(continued)*

spreads and funding costs have increased (see Figure 1.6, panel 2).

The Transmission Protection Instrument involves the purchases of public sector securities[1] issued

in jurisdictions in which disorderly and unwarranted market dynamics threaten monetary policy transmission. The instrument will be activated by the ECB's Governing Council based on a comprehensive assessment of market and transmission indicators and an evaluation of eligibility criteria.

---

[1]The ECB stated that it may consider purchases of private sector securities, if appropriate (see ECB 2022).

Box 1.3. Financial Markets and US Monetary Policy Tightening Cycles: A Historical Perspective

Over the past six decades, monetary policy tightening cycles in the United States have often been followed chronologically soon after by a recession. A well-cited exception is the 1994 cycle, when the Federal Reserve managed a so-called soft landing.[1] The magnitude of decline in economic activity, however, has varied considerably across recessionary periods (Figure 1.3.1). Given this background, the aim of this box is to examine the behavior of selected financial indicators during previous tighten-

ing cycles and identify any systematic trends of such variables that may help explain how the ongoing policy normalization cycle might play out in financial markets.[2]

Starting with cumulative increases in the policy rate, it appears that their magnitude has become more limited over each tightening cycle beginning with the 1988 episode, with a progressively lower terminal rate, likely reflecting in part a more muted inflationary environment compared to the 1970s and early 1980s.[3]

Figure 1.3.1. US Monetary Policy Tightening Cycles and Recessions, 1960 to Date
(Percent)

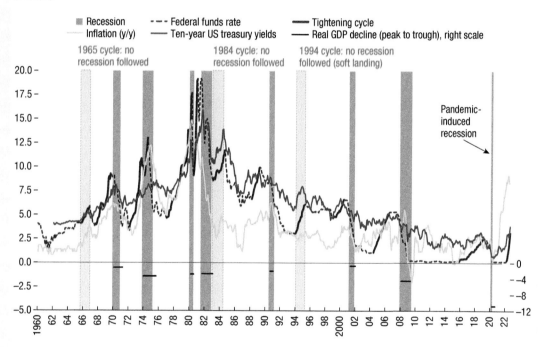

Sources: Bloomberg L.P.; Federal Reserve Economic Data; and IMF staff calculations.
Note: The tightening cycle periods are as defined in Blinder (2022). A soft landing is defined as a scenario in which the central bank tightens the policy rate—specifically, close to or above the neutral rate—and the economy does not fall into recession. Soft landings are shaded in light green. Inflation corresponds to year-over-year headline consumer price inflation. Gray shaded areas reflect recessions, as defined by the National Bureau of Economic Research. The 2022 tightening cycle is ongoing. y/y = year over year.

The authors of this box are Deepali Gautam, Sheheryar Malik, and Thomas Piontek.
[1] As noted in Powell (2022) there were three tightening cycles—1965, 1984, and 1994—during which the Federal Reserve "raised the federal funds rate significantly in response to perceived overheating without precipitating a recession."

[2] The objective of the box is not to forecast recessions but simply to understand how this tightening cycle compares with previous episodes through the lens of financial markets.
[3] The terminal rate corresponds to the level of policy rate reached at the peak of the tightening cycle. See Linde, Platzer, and Tietz (2022); Cesa-Bianchi, Harrison, and Sajedi (2022); and Rachel and Summers (2019) for a discussion of factors, in addition to inflationary pressures, that may be driving evolution of the terminal rate.

Box 1.3 *(continued)*

Figure 1.3.2. Evolution of Selected Financial Indicators during Tightening Cycles, United States, 1967–2022

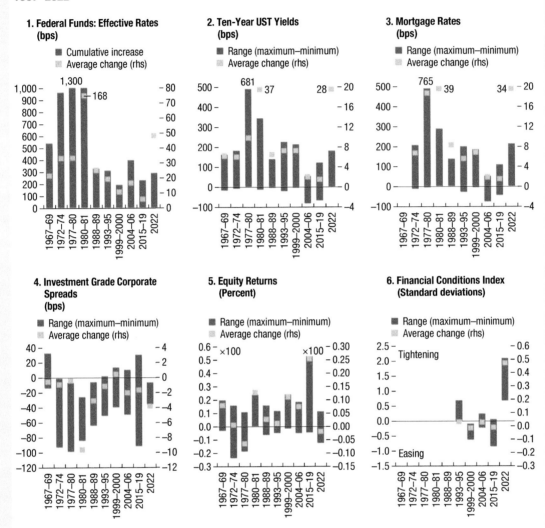

Sources: Bloomberg L.P.; Federal Reserve Economic Data; Freddie Mac; Moody's; and IMF staff calculations.
Note: Panel 1 shows the total increase in the federal funds rate over each tightening cycle, as well as its average monthly change (labeled "average change") denoted by the yellow markers. For variables considered in panels 2, 3, and 6, the green bars represent the range of maximum to minimum change in values from levels prevailing at the start of each respective tightening cycle. As in panel 1, the yellow markers denote the average monthly change over each cycle. Panel 3 shows percentage point changes in 30-year fixed-rate mortgages from Freddie Mac's Primary Mortgage Market Survey. Panel 4 shows spreads of Moody's Aaa corporate (investment-grade-rated) yields relative to 10-year US Treasury yields. Panel 5 shows the range of returns and average returns of the S&P 500 Index since the start of each cycle. The periods spanned by the tightening cycles are as defined in Blinder (2022). Data are not available for all tightening cycles considered for the financial conditions index and mortgage rates. bps = basis points; rhs = right scale; UST = US Treasury.

Importantly, the pace of current policy tightening to date is more comparable to episodes before 1988, as the Federal Reserve has moved aggressively to tackle inflation at decades-high levels (Figure 1.3.1 and Figure 1.3.2, panel 1). Longer-term interest rates have

generally moved upward across tightening cycles, although less so since the early 2000s, with the 10-year yield on US Treasuries trending down to record-low levels (Figure 1.3.1 and Figure 1.3.2, panel 2). But, consistent with the policy rate, the pace of increase in

Box 1.3 *(continued)*

the 10-year yield this time is more comparable to the cycles before 1988. The evolution of 30-year mortgage rates appears similar to that of the 10-year yield (Figure 1.3.2, panel 3). Risk assets such as equities and investment-grade corporate bonds have generally performed well during tightening cycles, even as the economy in many cases ended up in a recession afterward.[4] Investment-grade corporate spreads have typically compressed relative to the beginning of the tightening cycle, even though corporate bond yields have increased in sync with risk-free yields (Figure 1.3.2, panel 4). The magnitude of compression has tended to vary across cycles. The equity market has performed generally well across cycles, with the exception of the 1977–80 episode (Figure 1.3.2, panel 5) and the current cycle.[5] Financial conditions (as summarized by the IMF US financial conditions index) this time have tightened significantly compared to recent cycles, likely reflecting, in part, historically easy levels ahead of the tightening cycle (Figure 1.3.2, panel 6).

An important difference between the 1994 episode, which resulted in a soft landing, and the current tightening cycle, however, is the inflationary environment, as inflation during the former was significantly lower (Figure 1.3.1). In terms of inflation levels, the current period resembles more closely the 1970s and early 1980s, when recessions following tightening cycles were characterized by high inflation and low growth (so-called stagflation). In those episodes, a substantial rise in the policy rate was necessary to tame

inflation, followed by significant economic downturns. While the current inflationary environment may be reminiscent of the 1970s or early 1980s, the nature of the COVID-19 shock is unprecedented.[6] Moreover, the policy framework today is also very different. The Federal Reserve benefits from inflation-fighting credibility built over the past several decades, helping long-term inflation expectations remain much better anchored.[7] That said, financial vulnerabilities have emerged in some sectors in the wake of the COVID pandemic, and financial market volatility has notably risen after having remained relatively compressed over the preceding protracted period of low rates. The financial and regulatory architecture, however, has evolved considerably since the global financial crisis, and policymakers today have at their disposal a number of risk management tools that could be used to deal with the potential adverse systemic fallout from a disorderly tightening in financial conditions. With real rates still negative, and financial conditions still around neutral levels by historical standards (as shown in Figure 1.1), clear communication about the Federal Reserve's policy function—objectives, intertemporal trade-offs, and steps required to bring inflation credibly down to target—and the need to continue to normalize monetary policy remain crucial to avoid unwarranted market volatility and a disorderly tightening of financial conditions.

---

[4]During economic downturns, however, prices of risk assets have typically posted losses.

[5]It is more difficult to find a clear trend for the US dollar across tightening cycles given that other factors—including external factors that may not be directly affected by US tightening cycles—also influence its behavior.

[6]For a discussion relating to specific factors that may explain the recent uptrend in inflation—for example, the COVID-19 fiscal stimulus and stronger-than-anticipated demand related to the recovery—see the October 2022 *World Economic Outlook*, Box 1.1.

[7]Monetary policy transmission may also differ from the past given firms' higher concentration of market power and different labor market frictions, as discussed in the October 2022 *World Economic Outlook*, Box 1.2.

References

Abad, Jose, and Antonio Garcia Pascual. 2022. "Usability of Bank Capital Buffers: The Role of Market Expectations." IMF Working Paper 22/21, International Monetary Fund, Washington, DC.

Aronovich, Alex, and Andrew Meldrum. 2020. "New Financial Market Measures of the Neutral Real Rate and Inflation Expectations." FEDS Notes 2020–08–03, Board of Governors of the Federal Reserve System, Washington, DC.

Aronovich, Alex, and Andrew Meldrum. 2021. "High-Frequency Estimates of the Natural Real Rate and Inflation Expectations." Finance and Economics Discussion Series 2021–034, Board of Governors of the Federal Reserve System, Washington, DC.

Arslanalp, Serkan, Dimitris Drakopoulos, Rohit Goel, and Robin Koepke. 2020. "Benchmark-Driven Investments in Emerging Market Bond Markets." IMF Working Paper 20/192, International Monetary Fund, Washington, DC.

Blinder, Alan. 2022. "Landings Hard and Soft: The Fed, 1965–2020." Slides from a presentation delivered at the Bendheim Center for Finance, Princeton University, February 11.

Cesa-Bianchi, Ambrogio, Richard Harrison, and Rana Sajedi. 2022. "Decomposing the Drivers of Global R*." Staff Working Paper 990, Bank of England, London.

Christensen, Jens H. E., and James M. Gillan. 2022. "Does Quantitative Easing Affect Market Liquidity?" *Journal of Banking and Finance* 134 (2022).

Corwin, Shane A., and Paul Schultz. 2012. "A Simple Way to Estimate Bid-Ask Spreads from Daily High and Low Prices." *Journal of Finance* 67 (5): 719–59.

D'Amico, Stefania, Don H. Kim, and Min Wei. 2018. "Tips from TIPS: The Informational Content of Treasury Inflation-Protected Security Prices." *Journal of Financial and Quantitative Analysis* 53 (1): 395–436.

Del Negro, Marco, Domenico Giannone, Marc P. Giannoni, and Andrea Tambalotti. 2017. "Safety, Liquidity, and the Natural Rate of Interest." *Brookings Papers on Economic Activity* (Spring): 235–316.

European Central Bank (ECB). 2022. "The Transmission Protection Instrument." Press release, July 21.

Fernandez-Amador, Octavio, Martin Gächter, Martin Larch, and Georg Peter. 2013. "Does Monetary Policy Determine Stock Market Liquidity? New Evidence from the Euro Zone." *Journal of Empirical Finance* 21: 54–68.

Goel, Rohit, and Sheheryar Malik. 2021. "What Is Driving the Rise in Advanced Economy Bond Yields?" Global Financial Stability Note 21/03, International Monetary Fund, Washington, DC.

Gopinath, Gita. 2022. "How Will the Pandemic and War Shape Future Monetary Policy?" Speech at Jackson Hole Economic Policy Symposium, August 26.

Holston, Kathryn, Thomas Laubach, and John C. Williams. 2017. "Measuring the Natural Rate of Interest: International Trends and Determinants." *Journal of International Economics* 108 (Supplement 1): S59–S75.

International Monetary Fund (IMF). 2020. "The International Architecture for Resolving Sovereign Debt Involving Private-Sector Creditors—Recent Developments, Challenges, and Reform Options." IMF Policy Paper 20/043, Washington, DC.

International Monetary Fund (IMF). 2021. "Guidance Note for Developing Government Local Currency Bond Markets." IMF and World Bank Guidance Note 21/001, Washington, DC.

Johannsen, Benjamin K., and Elmar Mertens. 2016. "A Time Series Model of Interest Rates with the Effective Lower Bound." Finance and Economics Discussion Series 2016–033, Board of Governors of the Federal Reserve System, Washington, DC.

Kiley, Michael T. 2020. "What Can the Data Tell Us about the Equilibrium Real Interest Rate?" *International Journal of Central Banking* 16 (3): 181–209.

Linde, Jesper, Josef Platzer, and Robin Tietz. 2022. "Natural versus Neutral Rate of Interest: Parsing Disagreement about Future Short-Term Interest Rates." VoxEU.com, July 26.

Powell, Jerome H. 2022. "Restoring Price Stability." Speech delivered at Policy Options for Sustainable and Inclusive Growth–38th Annual Economic Policy Conference, National Association for Business Economics, March 21, Washington, DC.

Rachel, Lukasz, and Lawrence H. Summers. 2019. "On Falling Neutral Real Rates, Fiscal Policy, and the Risk of Secular Stagnation." *Brookings Papers on Economic Activity* (March).

Vitek, Francis. 2018. "The Global Macrofinancial Model." IMF Working Paper 18/081, International Monetary Fund, Washington, DC.

Wiggins, Kaye. 2022. "Selling to Yourself: The Private Equity Groups that Buy Companies They Own." *Financial Times*, June 21.

SCALING UP PRIVATE CLIMATE FINANCE IN EMERGING MARKET AND DEVELOPING ECONOMIES: CHALLENGES AND OPPORTUNITIES

Chapter 2 at a Glance

- Emerging market and developing economies account for two-thirds of global greenhouse gas emissions, and many are highly vulnerable to climate hazards. These economies will need significant climate financing in the coming years to reduce their emissions and to adapt to the physical effects of climate change.
- Private finance is key to achieving these objectives. Public budgets are strained in the wake of the COVID-19 crisis, and borrowing conditions for emerging market sovereigns have tightened (see Chapter 1).
- Establishing the right climate policies, including carbon pricing, remains crucial. Climate policies and finance are complementary—better policies incentivize private investment, which helps achieve policy objectives.
- The market for sustainable finance in emerging market and developing economies is advancing fast, particularly in Asia, as private investors increasingly look for investments with a positive climate impact.
- Significant challenges complicate efforts to scale up private climate finance in a decisive and timely manner, including a shortage of investable green projects. At the same time, fossil fuel investment remains high. Effective carbon pricing and a strong climate information architecture (data, disclosures, and taxonomies) are often lacking.
- Environmental, social, and governance (ESG) investments have grown rapidly, but their climate impact is unclear. Emerging market and developing economies are at a disadvantage from such investments because of systematically lower ESG scores and low investment allocations from ESG funds.
- Despite these challenges, there are various opportunities to scale up private climate finance. Harnessing them will require improvements on various fronts, as well as public support within overall budget constraints.
- Innovative financing instruments, such as emerging market green bond funds, can attract the necessary private institutional investors. Outcome-based debt instruments, such as sustainability-linked bonds, can also benefit emerging market issuers—if the key contractual aspects are set appropriately.
- Multilateral development banks and development finance institutions are crucial to help set up climate projects in low-income countries. They can also help design and implement innovative financial instruments to leverage private investment and provide risk absorption capacity. A larger share of equity finance by these institutions, combined with greater risk appetite and additional resources, would help achieve these objectives.
- Sovereign issuers have been latecomers to sustainable debt markets, but they can provide an important impetus for the development of private markets.
- Beyond shared principles for sustainable finance alignment approaches, the development of transition taxonomies allows emerging market issuers to send a clear signal of climate benefits to private investors—including in industries whose emissions are hard to abate. These are complementary to a stronger climate information architecture.
- The IMF supports its members through policy advice, identification of financial stability risks, capacity development, addressing data gaps, and advocacy for disclosure. Financing from the new Resilience and Sustainability Trust can help members address longer-term structural challenges, including climate change.

The authors of this chapter are Torsten Ehlers (co-lead), Charlotte Gardes-Landolfini (co-lead), Esti Kemp, Peter Lindner, and Yanzhe Xiao, under the supervision of Ananthakrishnan Prasad (unit chief, Climate Finance Policy) and Fabio Natalucci (deputy director).

Introduction

Emerging market and developing economies will need significant climate financing in coming years to reduce greenhouse gas emissions (mitigation finance) and adapt to the current and predicted physical effects of climate change (adaptation finance). The investment needs of these economies solely in renewable energy could reach $1 trillion a year by 2030 if they are to stay on track to achieve net-zero greenhouse gas emissions by 2050 (IEA 2021a).

Developing economies alone will require up to $300 billion a year by 2030 to adapt agriculture, infrastructure, water supply, and other parts of their economies to counterbalance the physical effects of climate change (UNEP 2021). If efforts to reduce emissions fall short of global temperature objectives set by the Paris Agreement, the need for adaptation financing will rise sharply for emerging market and developing economies. Estimates range from $520 billion to $1.75 trillion annually after 2050 depending on the emission pathway (Chapagain and others 2020).

The magnitude of emerging market and developing economy climate finance needs will require significant scaling up of private sources of finance. The public sector response to the COVID-19 pandemic has placed a burden on public finances in many of these economies, and borrowing costs are rising as central banks worldwide tighten policy to tackle high inflation (see Chapter 1). The issuance of private sustainable finance instruments in emerging market and developing economies thus far has held up relatively well, reflecting continued strong investor appetite. Yet private investment must at least double within this decade to cover the investment needs (Bhattacharya and others 2022).

Underinvestment in climate change mitigation and adaptation in emerging market and developing economies may lead to global financial stability risks through greater exposure to systemic climate-related financial risks. These economies already account for two-thirds of global emissions (IEA 2021b). Yet greater use of and investment in fossil-fuel-based energy systems from delayed decarbonization (carbon lock-in) may lead to cross-border and global spillover effects as a result of the negative externalities on global climate change and contagion effects along value chains.[1] In addition, because emerging market and developing economies include the majority of megadiverse countries, the loss of ecosystems strongly contributes to the impairment of carbon sinks, necessary to achieve global temperature objectives (NGFS 2022a). Many of these economies are also very vulnerable to climate hazards, with global hot spots in Africa, South Asia, Central and South America, and small island developing states. These vulnerabilities are amplified by poverty, governance challenges, violent conflicts, and a high share of livelihoods sensitive to climate change.

Scaling up private climate finance raises other fundamental challenges beyond the difficulties emerging market and developing economies already face in raising private finance more generally. These economies face a complex set of interwoven challenges to raise financing that have become more difficult to tackle since the COVID-19 pandemic—including the rise in government debt burdens, higher costs of capital, and underdeveloped banking sectors and capital markets (Prasad and others 2022). Climate finance, in particular adaptation finance, faces an even more fundamental problem: despite its significant benefits for society, it often does not generate sufficient private financial returns. Even if investors are comfortable with a higher level of credit risk, they often face an information asymmetry problem: ascertaining the potential climate benefits of their investments may not be possible with sufficient precision without robust climate data and disclosures. As a result, the risks associated with investing in emerging market and developing economy assets are often deemed too high, deterring otherwise reportedly strong investor interest in sustainable assets. It is unclear whether the very large and quickly growing environmental, social, and governance (ESG) investment flows could play a significant role in scaling up private climate finance. In addition to the still uncertain climate benefits of ESG investing, emerging market and developing economy firms' ESG scores are systematically lower than those for firms from advanced markets, and investment funds with an ESG

---

[1] Carbon lock-in is a specific type of path dependence that occurs when fossil-fuel-intensive systems delay or prevent the low-carbon transition. It is driven by a complex interaction of persistent institutional, market, and policy failures that inhibit the diffusion of low-carbon technologies despite their apparent climate, environmental, and economic advantages.

focus allocate significantly fewer funds to emerging market assets.

At the same time, there are various opportunities to scale up private climate finance beyond generally improving the investment environment in emerging market and developing economies. Harnessing these opportunities will require improvements on several fronts. Innovative types of structured finance and out-come-based financial instruments that can overcome some of the challenges will need to be deployed on a larger scale and improved where necessary. Transi-tion finance taxonomies, which determine whether and how assets are aligned with emission-reduction goals, would benefit emerging market and devel-oping economy issuers by better signaling current and future climate benefits—even for industries with currently high emissions. The climate infor-mation architecture—comprising data, disclosures, and taxonomies to align investments with climate goals—requires strengthening (IMF 2021b; NGFS 2022b). The public sector, including multilateral development banks (MDBs), development finance institutions (DFIs), and other international financial institutions—such as the IMF—must play a key role in crowding in private climate financing in emerg-ing market and developing economies, including by placing more emphasis on equity rather than debt financing. Sovereign issuers have been latecomers—and even absent—from sustainable finance markets, but they can boost market development. The United Nations Framework Convention on Climate Change (UNFCCC) carbon markets could generate sig-nificant investment flows to emerging market and developing economies for mitigation purposes, if they are fully implemented. At the same time, specialized vehicles, such as the Green Climate Fund, will need sufficient funding to support adaptation finance.[2]

The International Monetary Fund (IMF) can also play an important role, including through its new Resilience and Sustainability Trust (RST). The IMF can help strengthen the climate information archi-tecture and support emerging market and developing economies with the design and implementation of supportive climate policies, including carbon pricing.

RST financing could help eligible and qualifying emerging market and developing economies tackle longer-term structural challenges from climate change by providing affordable long-term financing and helping catalyze (public and) private financing. The RST could also be tapped to develop a conducive investment climate by promoting reform measures to improve the regulatory environment and increase the resilience of the infrastructure needed to address climate change.

Although this chapter focuses on financial markets and instruments as ways to overcome existing chal-lenges for climate finance in emerging market and developing economies, implementing the necessary and appropriate climate policies remains crucial. Climate policies and finance are complementary—climate policies are a prerequisite for enabling private finance, which in turn contributes to the achievement of climate policy goals.[3] Carbon pricing is an effective tool to make high emitters pay for the climate costs they cause and thereby channel investment toward projects that emit less.[4] More generally, climate policies and commitments, such as the Nationally Determined Contributions under the Paris Agreement, send a strong signal to investors. This can help direct invest-ment flows to support the transition to a low-carbon economy.

The Market for Private Climate Finance in Emerging Market and Developing Economies: Moving toward the Mainstream

Sustainable finance markets in emerging market and developing economies, particularly in Asia, have become progressively more mainstream, and 2021 was a breakout year. Although green bonds are still the main instrument in the sustainable finance eco-system in emerging market and developing econo-mies (59 percent in 2022 to date), other sustainable

---

[2]The Green Climate Fund was established in 2010 under the UNFCCC framework to limit or reduce greenhouse gas emissions in developing economies. The fund maintains a 50/50 balance between mitigation and adaptation finance.

[3]The recently legislated US Inflation Reduction Act is an example of a policy that incentivizes private investments in carbon-neutral energy production through tax credits.

[4]The IMF's October 2019 *Fiscal Monitor* emphasizes the impor-tance of carbon taxes and pricing to the implementation of carbon mitigation strategies. The IMF's October 2020 *World Economic Outlook* argues that steadily rising carbon prices in combination with a green investment push can deliver the needed emission reductions at reasonable cost. See also www.imf.org/en/Topics/climate-change/climate-mitigation.

Figure 2.1. The Momentum for Sustainable Finance Remains Strong in Emerging Market and Developing Economies, with Notable Differences in Instruments and Regional Composition

Sustainable debt issuance in EMDEs grew strongly in 2021, with a notable rise in sustainability-linked instruments.

1. Sustainable Instrument Issuance in EMDEs, by Type
(Billions of US dollars; percent)

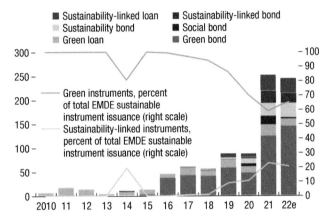

Much of this growth has been driven by issuance in the Asia-Pacific region.

2. Share of Sustainable Instruments in EMDEs and Territorial Greenhouse Gas Emissions by Region, 2021
(Percent of GDP; tCO$_2$e per million US dollars of GDP)

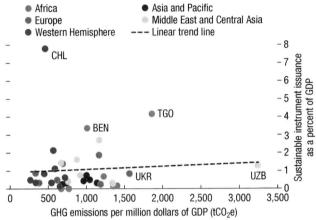

Despite recent increases, sustainable debt issuance remains limited in EMDEs, with some exceptions.

3. Issuance of Sustainable Instruments as a Percent of GDP
(Percent)

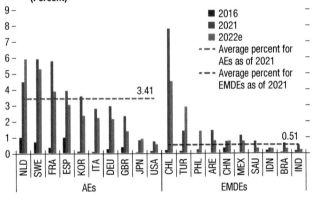

Maturities vary substantially across instruments.

4. Sustainable Instrument Initial Maturity in EMDEs by Type
(Year)

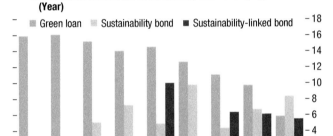

Sources: Bloomberg Finance L.P.; Emissions Database for Paris Reality Check; Eora Global Supply Chain Database; IMF, World Economic Outlook database; and IMF staff calculations.
Note: Data for 2022 in panels 1 and 3 are annualized based on the first half of 2022 (2022e). Panel 3 shows countries filtered by sustainable instrument issuance amounts in 2022 among AEs and EMDEs separately. Panels 2 and 3 use International Organization for Standardization (ISO) country codes. AE = advanced economy; e = estimate; EMDE = emerging market and developing economy; GHG = greenhouse gas; tCO$_2$e = metric tons of carbon dioxide equivalent.

finance debt instruments (social, sustainability, and sustainability-linked loans and bonds) have gained prominence since 2018, especially outside of China (Figure 2.1, panel 1).[5] Variation is notable across

regions (Figure 2.1, panel 2). The Asia-Pacific region has dominated emerging market and developing economy debt issuance, with 60 percent of sustainable issuance in 2021 and 72 percent in 2022 to date, in line with the region's large share of

---

[5]Green bond instruments are regular financial instruments whose proceeds are used to finance projects that benefit the environment (such as solar energy projects). Social bonds must be used to finance social projects (such as affordable housing), while sustainability bonds finance a combination of green and

social projects. All three are "use-of-proceeds" instruments. For sustainability-linked instruments, the issuer sets a contractual target for the borrower to achieve sustainability goals (such as reducing greenhouse gas emissions), with free use of proceeds.

Figure 2.2. The Development of Private Climate Finance Comes with a Series of Challenges

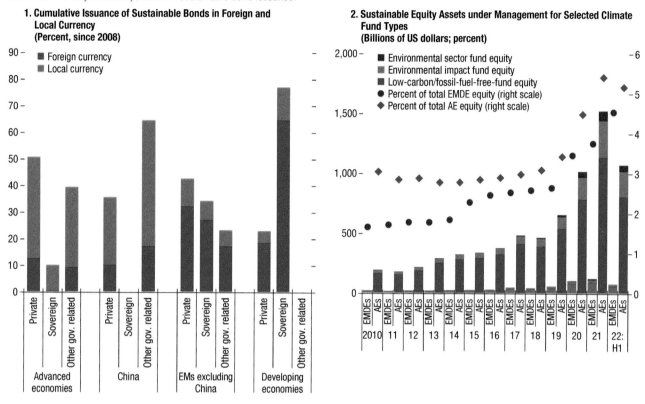

China, emerging markets excluding China, and developing economies have followed very different patterns in sustainable bond issuance.

Despite recent increases, sustainable equity investments remain small.

1. Cumulative Issuance of Sustainable Bonds in Foreign and Local Currency
(Percent, since 2008)

2. Sustainable Equity Assets under Management for Selected Climate Fund Types
(Billions of US dollars; percent)

Sources: Bloomberg Finance L.P.; Morningstar Direct; and IMF staff calculations.
Note: Data for 2022 in panel 1 are annualized based on the first half of 2022. Panel 1 includes only sustainable bonds (excluding US municipal bonds). "Private" includes bonds issued by financial institutions as well as industrial, renewable energy, and utilities bonds. "Sovereign" includes bonds issued by central governments. "Other gov. related" includes bonds issued by agencies and local authorities, as well as covered bonds (debt instruments secured by a cover pool of mortgage loans or public sector debt on which investors have a preferential claim in the event of default). Country classifications in panel 1 are mutually exclusive. Data in panel 2 are as of the first half of 2022. Detailed definitions of variables in panel 2 can be found in Online Annex 2.1. AE = advanced economy; EM = emerging market; EMDE = emerging market and developing economy.

emissions—about 60 percent of emerging market and developing economies' total territorial emissions. While China remains a significant player, other emerging market and developing economies—especially Chile, India, Mexico, and Türkiye—have seen a sharp pickup in the issuance of sustainable debt as a share of GDP since 2016.

However, the issuance of sustainable debt in emerging market and developing economies remains a small share of GDP and lower than that of advanced economies (Figure 2.1, panel 3). Maturities vary across instrument types and have shrunk as issuance has grown—except for sustainability bonds (Figure 2.1, panel 4)—due to headwinds in emerging market debt markets more generally.

Issuance of sustainable bonds follows very different issuer patterns across regions. Sovereign issuance has been absent in China and accounted for only 10 percent of all issuances (since 2008) in advanced economies (Figure 2.2, panel 1). The share has been much larger in emerging markets excluding China (34 percent) and developing economies (77 percent). Issuance by other entities—mainly government agencies and local authorities—has totaled 64 percent in China and 39 percent in advanced economies. These high shares reflect greater reliance on public institutions at the local level in the financing of green infrastructure projects in China and the United States. While the share of private sector issuance in other emerging markets, at 43 percent, is comparable to the share in advanced economies and China, it is much lower in developing economies at 23 percent.

The low share of private sector issuance in developing economies and the high share of foreign currency issuance in emerging market and developing economies may be explained by a lack of depth in domestic capital markets, including the small scale of local currency bond markets, and high credit risk. The high share of foreign currency issuance in emerging market and developing economies appears to reflect demand for sustainable bonds driven largely by investors based in advanced economies who prefer hard currency over local currency debt. For developing economies, another significant factor is the relative lack of corporations large enough to issue bonds, especially in the global markets.

Sustainable equity allocations of investment funds to emerging market and developing economies remain small despite recent increases. As a share of total equity assets under management, however, the difference between advanced and emerging market and developing economies is much smaller (Figure 2.2, panel 2, blue diamonds and red circles).

Challenges for Scaling Up Private Climate Finance in Emerging Market and Developing Economies

Despite the increasing momentum behind private climate finance in emerging market and developing economies, several challenges remain when it comes to significantly scaling up financing. These include the complexities of matching the supply and demand of financing, various institutional and informational constraints holding back projects and financing, a lack of effective carbon pricing, still-strong fossil fuel investment, an underdeveloped climate information architecture, and features of ESG scores and funds that put these economies at a disadvantage.

The Climate Financing Gap Remains Large, and Matching the Sources of Supply with Demand Is Complex

The mismatch between emerging market and developing economies' climate financing needs and current investment flows has produced a large financing gap. For purposes of climate mitigation, infrastructure

financing—mainly in the transport and energy sectors—falls short of needs across all regions (Figure 2.3, panel 1). The relative financing gap is even greater for adaptation purposes, particularly for water and sanitation, irrigation, and flood protection, where investment is almost nonexistent (Figure 2.3, panel 2). It is even more concerning that the more important a region's aggregated vulnerability to climate change (measured by its exposure, sensitivity, and ability to adapt), the greater the financing gap. Financing needs for mitigation and adaptation purposes are also large relative to GDP across all regions (Figure 2.3, panel 3). It is therefore critical for the international community to meet or even exceed the goal of providing $100 billion in climate finance to developing economies each year and to make sure a sizable amount of the climate finance goes to adaptation. At the same time, carbon pricing initiatives, still nascent in those economies, offer only limited price signals to support climate financing (Figure 2.3, panel 4).

Addressing this mismatch is challenging given the current structure of climate finance markets. In terms of instruments, sustainable finance markets remain largely dominated by debt, which has about twice as large a share as equity financing (60 percent versus 32 percent of total climate finance; see Online Annex 2.2). With respect to sources of financing and types of intermediaries, the private sector—commercial financial institutions, funds, households, and corporations—accounts for about half of the flows. All types of financing instruments and investors, with different investment horizons, needs for scale, risk profiles, and funding sources, need to be mobilized for mitigation and adaptation purposes. For instance, renewable energy infrastructure and low-carbon technologies (such as carbon capture and storage, batteries, low-carbon hydrogen) will largely require equity finance (IEA 2021a).

At the same time, several constraints hold back projects and financing on the supply and demand sides. Investors have noted various reasons for gaps in financing needs related to lack of investable projects (Ehlers 2014; Fouad and others 2021). They point to bottlenecks in project preparation and development. Deficiencies in policy and regulatory frameworks and weaker institutional capacity (related to contract enforcement, property rights, and management of fiscal risks and public investment) make it hard to manage the long-term investments needed in sustainable infrastructure. In addition, investors point to a need for high-quality, reliable, and comparable data.

Figure 2.3. A Deep-Seated Financing Gap for Climate Change Mitigation and Adaptation, Limited Fiscal Capacity, and Carbon Pricing Strategies in Emerging Market and Developing Economies

The overall gap vis-à-vis mitigation needs is high across regions ...

... and even more so for adaptation finance, despite the high level of vulnerabilities to climate change.

1. Global Climate Finance Flows in Mitigation and Infrastructure Investment Needs by Region
(Billions of US dollars)

- Private
- Public: multilateral development financial institutions
- Public: others
- Gap vis-à-vis annual infrastructure investment need (preferred scenario)

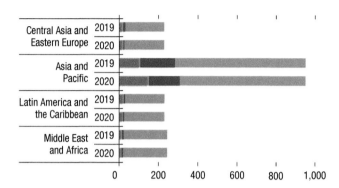

2. Global Climate Finance Flows in Adaptation, Infrastructure Investment Needs, and Vulnerability Score by Region
(Billions of US dollars, bottom; score, top)

- Private
- Public: others
- Gap vis-à-vis annual infrastructure investment need (preferred scenario)
- Public: multilateral development financial institutions
- GDP-weighted average vulnerability score (top scale)

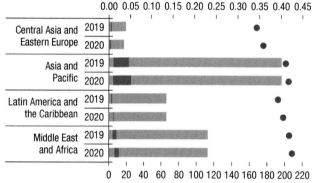

Needs relative to GDP are significant across regions, specifically in Central Asia and Eastern Europe and in Middle East and Africa.

However, carbon pricing initiatives remain nascent in those economies, with insufficiencies in coverage and rates.

3. Annual Infrastructure Investment Needs Relative to GDP
(Percent of GDP; billions of 2015 US dollars)

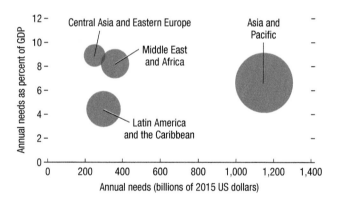

4. National and Subnational Carbon Pricing Initiatives as a Share of National Greenhouse Gas Emissions with Average Price Rate
(Percent of national greenhouse gas emissions; US dollars per tCO$_2$e)

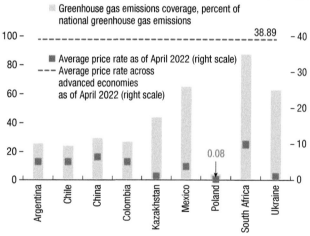

Sources: Climate Policy Initiative (2021); Emissions Database for Global Atmospheric Research; Emissions Database for Paris Reality Check; Eora Global Supply Chain Database; Notre Dame Global Adaptation Index; World Bank (2019); World Bank Carbon Pricing database; World Economic Outlook database; and IMF staff calculations.
Note: In panels 1 and 2, the infrastructure needs for mitigation include the energy and transport sectors, and infrastructure needs for adaptation include the water and sanitation, irrigation, and flood protection sectors. The climate finance flow includes both emerging market and developing economies and advanced economies in selected regions; the infrastructure investment needs are calculated for all low- and middle-income countries. Therefore, the infrastructure needs gap is underestimated. In panel 2, the GDP-weighted average vulnerability score measures a country's exposure, sensitivity, and capacity to adapt to negative effects of climate change. "Private" category is too small to be displayed (always below 1 billion US dollars). In panel 3, the size of the bubble represents the GDP. In panel 4, "price rate" is the cost per tCO$_2$e emissions from both the carbon tax and emission trading system. The coverage of each carbon pricing initiative is presented as a share of annual national greenhouse gas emissions for 2021. Detailed variable definitions can be found in Online Annex 2.1. tCO$_2$e = metric ton of carbon dioxide equivalent.

Figure 2.4. Debt Levels of Emerging Market and Developing Economy Companies Operating in Fossil Fuel Industries Continue to Increase

Debt levels of companies headquartered in Asia and the Middle East have increased at the highest rate ...

... while debt levels of companies pursuing expansion plans have also increased, notably in Asia.

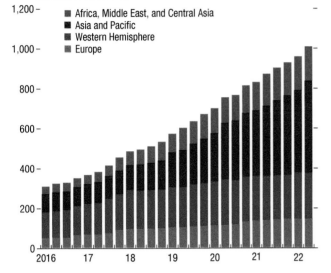

1. **Total Debt of Companies Operating in the Oil and Gas Industry Domiciled in EMDEs**
   (Billions of US dollars)

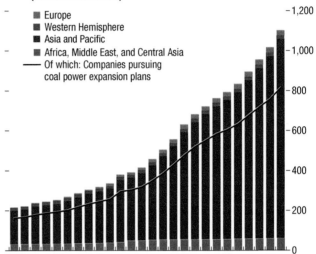

2. **Total Debt of Companies with a Significant Role in the Thermal Coal Value Chain Domiciled in EMDEs**
   (Billions of US dollars)

Sources: Bloomberg Finance L.P.; Urgewald; and IMF staff calculations.
Note: Companies in panel 1 include those with expansion activities in the upstream and midstream sectors. Total debt includes bonds and loans. Data are based on a sample of roughly 80 companies for which debt statistics are available from 2016 onward, out of 250 identified companies headquartered in EMDEs. Companies in panel 2 include those meeting criteria set out by Urgewald. Total debt includes bonds and loans. Data are based on a sample of 106 parent companies and subsidiaries for which debt statistics are available from 2016 onward, out of roughly 2,200 identified that are headquartered in EMDEs. The sample represents roughly 25 percent of the installed coal power capacity of companies headquartered in EMDEs. Companies with expansion plans are those planning to develop new coal-fired power capacity of at least 100 megawatts. EMDE = emerging market and developing economy.

The Triple Challenge: The Lack of Carbon Pricing and Fossil Fuel Investment and an Underdeveloped Climate Information Architecture

Currently, emerging market and developing economies lag advanced economies in their implementation of carbon pricing. Nascent initiatives—mainly carbon taxes—fall short of targets both in emission coverage and prices when compared with advanced economies (Figure 2.3, panel 4). Consumption subsidies for fossil fuels in some emerging market and developing economies are essentially a persistent form of negative carbon pricing, which makes for an uneven playing field for investments in low-carbon technologies.

Investment in emerging market and developing economies is still tilted toward the fossil fuel sector, which has experienced a substantial rebound in debt issuance since the Paris Agreement. In the coal sector, the growth of outstanding debt (bonds and loans) was more than 400 percent between the first quarter of 2016 and the second quarter of 2022, with a nearly 500 percent increase in the Asia-Pacific region (Figure 2.4). The ability to raise debt financing has also been high in the oil and gas sector, where outstanding debt grew 225 percent, with a more than 400 percent increase in the Asia-Pacific region over the same period (primarily via bank loans). Moreover, debt of companies in emerging market and developing economies with coal power expansion plans increased about 350 percent between 2016 and 2022; annual growth in the second quarter of 2022 was nearly 30 percent. This increase occurred despite caution that an achievement of net-zero emission targets requires halting new oil and gas field development, new coal mines, and extensions beyond projects already committed to as of 2021 (IEA 2021a). Against this backdrop, Russia's war in Ukraine and the move away from Russian energy in Europe could result in a significant setback, incentivizing further fossil fuel exploration in emerging market and developing economies.

Further, the climate information architecture in emerging market and developing economies remains underdeveloped despite recent advances. There is a lack of granular, quality climate data in these economies, and there are challenges in terms of both availability and accessibility. Data sets on climate variables (for example, temperature and precipitation) and carbon intensity are sparse, especially for Africa, small island developing states, and regions in high-mountain Asia (NGFS 2022b). While climate-related corporate disclosures have recently improved—mostly across Asia, Chile, Peru, South Africa, and Türkiye—disclosures remain voluntary in most countries and lack standardization, consistency, and reliability because of an absence of auditing requirements. Current disclosures cannot give a consistent picture of financial sector exposure to climate-related risks and opportunities because of the lack of high-quality, consistent, and comparable climate data.

The Chinese and European taxonomies have propelled several emerging market and developing economies—primarily in Asia and Latin America—to develop their own regional or national taxonomies. The taxonomies of the Association of Southeast Asian Nations (ASEAN), as well as Indonesia, Malaysia, and Singapore (via a "traffic light" approach),[6] are notable examples of transition taxonomies. They aim to identify improvements in emissions over time and across sectors, including within the most carbon-intensive sectors, to support the transition to a low-carbon economy. Nonetheless, most existing taxonomy projects have still not been tested for robustness to meet long-term temperature goals and for their impact on financial markets, including by potentially diverting investment from carbon-intensive activities or companies facing complex transitions. As for global initiatives such as the International Platform

on Sustainable Finance's Common Ground Taxonomy and regulations and policies in advanced economies (primarily Europe and the United States), the impact on emerging market and developing economies is unclear at this point; these initiatives could, however, serve as benchmarks for capital market development in these economies.

Environmental, Social, and Governance Scores and Investment Funds Put Emerging Market and Developing Economy Firms at a Disadvantage

ESG investing is a major and growing investment trend, but its impact on climate finance in emerging market and developing economies may be limited. The Global Sustainable Investment Alliance estimates that the assets under management of funds with an ESG-related investment mandate have reached $35.3 trillion, or about 36 percent of global assets under management (GSIA 2020). About half of ESG funds' assets are allocated to equities (52 percent at the end of the second quarter of 2022). A small increase in the share of ESG fund allocations to emerging market and developing economies could in principle result in significant investment flows.

A general challenge for ESG scores and investing, however, is the lack of focus on ESG impact, including climate change. ESG scores are based on a large number (usually more than 100) of ESG-related data points, such as whether a firm has a carbon transition plan (an E component). Typically, a higher ESG score indicates better ESG "performance" of a firm.[7] Recent IMF research, however, finds that there is limited scope for investment strategies based on ESG indicators to meaningfully help mitigate climate change (Elmalt, Kirti, and Igan 2021). Historically, ESG ratings evolved as a means to manage non-financial risks, rather than to assess the ESG benefits of firms.[8] Recent scrutiny around the labeling of

---

[6]A traffic light approach means that an economic activity may be characterized as green, amber, or red, depending on its contribution to climate change mitigation, according to a series of technology- and emission-related criteria.

[7]For some providers the opposite is the case. One prominent example is Sustainalytics (owned by Morningstar), for which a higher score represents a higher ESG risk and therefore lower ESG "performance." See www.sustainalytics.com/esg-data.

[8]Indeed, the most prominent ESG rating providers clearly state that their scores are risk ratings. For MSCI, the largest ESG rating provider by market share, see www.msci.com/our -solutions/esg-investing/esg-ratings/what-esg-ratings-are-and-are -not. For Sustainalytics, the second largest, see www.sustainalytics .com/esg-data.

Figure 2.5. ESG Scores and Fund Allocations Are Systematically Lower for Firms in Emerging Market and Developing Economies

The distribution of ESG scores of firms is dominated by scores for firms listed in advanced economies.

This skewing cannot be explained by the size of EMDE firms, which on average does not differ from advanced economy firms in the sample.

1. Smoothed Distribution Function of ESG Scores (Probability)

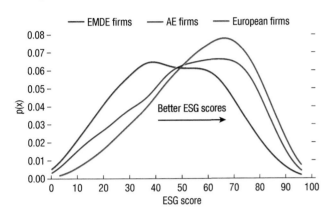

2. ESG Scores and Firm Size

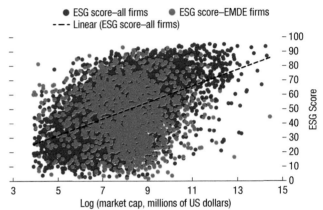

Allocations of ESG funds to EMDEs are lower than those of other funds ...

... which is driven partly by the relatively small size of ESG funds dedicated to EMDEs.

3. Share of EMDE Allocations of ESG vs. Other Funds (Percent)

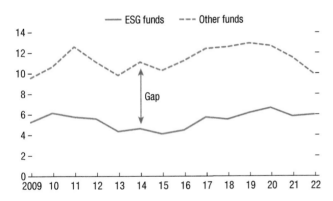

4. EMDE-Dedicated ESG Funds vs. EMDE Non-ESG Funds (Billions of US dollars; percent)

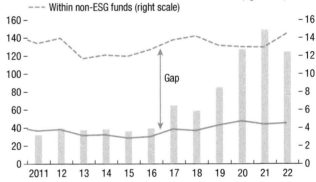

Sources: Morningstar; Refinitiv; and IMF staff calculations.
Note: Panels 1 and 2 are based on listed firms only—more than 6,200 in total, of which more than 1,300 are from EMDEs. Panel 1 excludes US firms for the Refinitiv ESG scores because the data have a bias toward covering small US firms and penalize these firms for not reporting E data. This is not the case for most other ESG rating providers. Panel 1 shows a smoothed distribution function of the ESG scores. A higher score implies better ESG performance. Panels 3 and 4 include data up to the end of second quarter of 2022. AE = advanced economy; AUM = assets under management; EM = emerging market; EMDE = emerging market and developing economy; ESG = environmental, social, and governance.

ESG funds further suggests that not all ESG funds sufficiently incorporate ESG factors into their investment strategies.

ESG scores appear to be systematically lower for emerging market and developing economy firms than for advanced economy firms. While the distribution of ESG scores from different providers can differ significantly (Berg, Kölbel, and Rigobon 2022), listed emerging market and developing economy firms tend

to have, on average, lower scores than their advanced economy counterparts (Figure 2.5, panel 1). This is true also for the individual E, S, and G scores (see Online Annex 2.6 for a more detailed analysis of ESG scores). One determinant of ESG scores appears to be firm size (Drempetic, Klein, and Zwergel 2020). In the data sample of listed firms, however, emerging market and developing economy firms, on average, are not significantly smaller than advanced economy firms (Figure 2.5, panel 2). Online Annex 2.6 contains a more formal regression analysis, showing that in addition to size, industry composition, firms' financial performance, and other unobserved firm characteristics cannot fully account for the lower ESG scores of these economies' firms.[9] These results also hold true for E scores only. Which ESG characteristics can account for the systematically lower scores of emerging market and developing economy firms is difficult to pinpoint. A large number of data points are used to construct ESG scores, and these data points differ depending on the industry. Further, the individual ESG characteristics that feed into the scores, and the weight they receive, are at the discretion of ESG scoring providers and vary substantially across providers.

Allocations to emerging market and developing economies (equities and bonds) by ESG investment funds are also lower than those by non-ESG funds (Figure 2.5, panel 3).[10] One reason for the significant and persistent difference is the lack of ESG funds dedicated to these economies (Figure 2.5, panel 4). But emerging market and developing economy allocations between ESG funds and other funds also differ for global funds that invest in both advanced and emerging market and developing economies (see Online Annex 2.7).[11]

Harnessing the Opportunities to Scale Up Private Climate Finance in Emerging Market and Developing Economies

Given the scale and variety of climate investment needs, a single instrument or approach is unlikely to be sufficient or advisable. The opportunities discussed in this chapter present a set of feasible and complementary tools for different use cases and country circumstances.

---

[9]Another potential explanation is the lack of reporting of ESG data, which induces a penalty in the analyzed ESG data. This is, however, not the case for all ESG scoring providers.

[10]The difference in allocations to emerging market and developing economies between ESG and non-ESG funds holds true separately for equities and bonds. See Online Annex 2.7. All online annexes are available at www.imf.org/en/Publications/GFSR.

[11]A link between systematically lower scores of emerging market firms and low ESG fund allocations to these economies' assets is suggestive, but it is difficult to establish it formally. To what extent ESG funds use ESG scores (and from which providers) in determining their investment allocations is typically not publicized. Further, ESG funds often combine the use of ESG scores with other criteria to determine their asset allocations.

Innovative Financing Instruments and the Role of Multilateral Development Banks

Innovation in climate finance has proceeded rapidly, including four distinct types of instruments and approaches that address different fundamental challenges and therefore have different use cases (Table 2.1 and Online Annex 2.4). *Structured finance vehicles* purchase green bonds from emerging market banks and target large institutional investors. MDBs purchase equity or provide a credit risk guarantee to these structures to reduce the risks such that pension funds or insurance companies can invest. *Blended finance* more broadly combines public and donor capital to de-risk infrastructure investments for private capital, thereby helping to mobilize and scale up climate private finance. *Outcome-based sustainable debt instruments*, such as sustainability-linked bonds, include an incentive mechanism to address information asymmetries between issuers and investors (called "greenwashing," when sustainability benefits of investments are not as high as issuers claim). In *"pay-for-success" private financing* for public sector projects, third-party investors, including private investors, provide the initial investment and develop a project. The public sector then purchases the project for an amount linked to the project's sustainability performance—investors receive higher compensation with higher performance measured by indicators agreed on in advance.

The public sector, including MDBs and DFIs, has an important role to play in employing some of these instruments.[12] To attract private capital, the various risks associated with emerging market and developing economy financial assets (ranging from credit, foreign exchange, and macroeconomic risks to governance and political risks) must be reduced. National development banks, MDBs, and DFIs can efficiently employ their resources and expertise to crowd in private finance. By absorbing a portion of these risks, providing technical assistance and capacity development, and lending their reputation and expertise, these institutions can play an important role in attracting private investors that would not otherwise have provided funding for climate-beneficial

---

[12]Unlike MDBs, which provide financial assistance to promote economic and social development, DFIs are specialized development banks or subsidiaries set up specifically to support *private* sector development. These are usually majority-owned institutions of national governments and source their capital from national or international development funds or benefit from government guarantees.

Table 2.1. Selected Innovative Financial Instruments for Climate Finance

Type of Instrument	Structured Finance and EMDE (Closed-End) Fixed-Income Funds	Blended Finance for Infrastructure and Other Complex Projects	Outcome-Based Sustainable Debt Instruments	Private Finance for Public Sector Projects ("Pay for Success")
Examples	Green bond funds: IFC-Amundi; Axa's Blue Like an Orange (in progress)	Equity, mezzanine/first-loss finance for infrastructure projects	Sustainability-linked instruments (bonds, loans, commercial paper, etc.)	Environmental impact "bonds"
Description	Green bonds issued by EMDE banks (against green loans) are securitized into green bonds with the public sector providing credit risk reduction	MDBs or the public sector make an equity or mezzanine investment, or provide a guarantee to de-risk and crowd in private investors	Issuer receives a bonus (pays a penalty) if sustainability target agreed on in advance (based on clearly defined indicators) is met (missed)	Contract with a public sector authority that pays if predefined environmental outcomes are achieved
Use case	Emerging markets with existing bank loans to green projects	New infrastructure projects (for example, in the energy sector); use of new types of technologies with potentially higher risks; agriculture	Support firm-level or government-level alignment with sustainability targets (such as greenhouse-gas-emission reductions)	Adaptation finance, nonbankable transition finance
Fundamental challenges addressed	Reduction in credit risk (through elevation to investment-grade finance), scaling, diversification, potential currency risk reduction through pooling	Mitigation of credit and political risks; mitigation of information asymmetry problems	Information asymmetry ("greenwashing")	Capacity limits in developing complex green projects (such as in infrastructure); potential inefficiencies in public sector investment
Targeted private investors	Institutional investors, including pension funds and insurance companies	Specialist investors and investment funds; local investors	All	Specialized funds, donor funds, MDBs
Mechanism to ensure climate benefits	Selection of eligible bank loans; usual green bond certification	Project selection and technical assistance	Bonus (or penalty) provides incentive to fulfill sustainability target	Project selection; due diligence
Public sector/ MDB involvement	De-risking (purchase equity tranche/provide first-loss guarantee); technical assistance	Own resources for equity/ mezzanine investment and guarantees; provide specialized expertise for project design	None. Sovereigns could issue to support market development and set standards	Direct investment; technical assistance
Design/incentive issues	Requires existing bank loans and technical assistance for banks to issue green bonds	Complex contractual agreements; extensive equity/mezzanine investment and guarantees can create moral hazard; limits returns for other equity investors	Sustainability targets may not be sufficiently ambitious; penalties need to be high enough to motivate issuer to achieve target	High financial and political risks for private investors
Potential to scale up finance	High	Limited by public sector MDB resources	Limited by issuer characteristics	Limited by fiscal resources

Source: IMF staff illustration.

Note: EMDE = emerging market and developing economy; MDB = multilateral development bank.

Figure 2.6. Multilateral Development Banks Have Scope to Draw in More Private Climate Finance for Emerging Market and Developing Economies

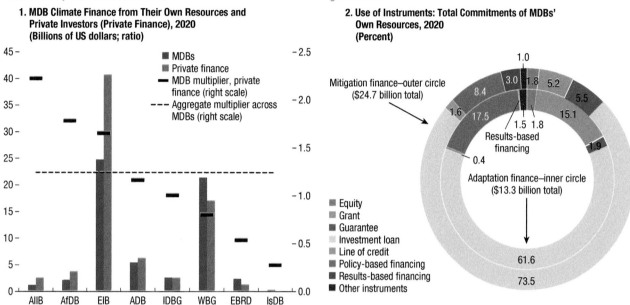

MDBs crowd in private finance on average of only about 1.2 times the resources they commit themselves ...

... in part because they invest a small share in equity instruments or guarantees.

1. MDB Climate Finance from Their Own Resources and Private Investors (Private Finance), 2020
(Billions of US dollars; ratio)

2. Use of Instruments: Total Commitments of MDBs' Own Resources, 2020
(Percent)

Sources: World Bank, *2020 Joint Report on Multilateral Development Banks' Climate Finance*; and IMF staff calculations.
Note: Commitments include the nominal value of guarantees, which may or may not lead to use of a multilateral development bank's own resources. ADB = Asian Development Bank; AfDB = African Development Bank; AIIB = Asian Infrastructure Investment Bank; EBRD = European Bank for Reconstruction and Development; EIB = European Investment Bank; IDBG = Inter-American Development Bank Group; IsDB = Islamic Development Bank; MDB = multilateral development bank; WBG = World Bank Group.

investments in emerging market and developing economies. Naturally, this entails risks for the public sector, which need to be managed appropriately (Prasad and others 2022).

The emerging market green bond fund established by the International Finance Corporation (IFC) and asset manager Amundi exemplifies efficient use of MDB resources to attract private finance. The fund (AP EGO) set up by Amundi pooled green bonds issued by banks in various emerging market and developing economies. It thereby leveraged on the expertise of local banks and their critical role as a source of financing in these economies. The IFC, part of the World Bank Group, purchased a first-loss/equity tranche of the green bond fund. This reduced the credit risk for other investors to what is called "investment-grade level," allowing pension funds to invest (see Online Annex 2.5). IFC's equity investment of $125 million enabled a fund totaling $2 billion, a multiple of 16 (Bolton, Musca, and Samama 2020).

MDB resources could be targeted more to attracting private sector climate finance. On average, MDBs attracted only 1.2 times the amount of private finance (equity and debt) relative to commitments of their own resources in 2020 (Figure 2.6, panel 1). There is an ongoing and long-standing discussion about how to leverage the resources of MDBs most efficiently for climate finance (Basu and others 2011). The use of equity has the greatest potential to maximize co-financing because it enables a potentially high multiple of additional debt finance. The use of equity, however, remains very limited, at about 1.8 percent of total MDB commitments to private climate finance in emerging market and developing economies (Figure 2.6, panel 2).

Scaling up MDB commitments significantly would ultimately require an expansion of their own resources for climate finance. Developing climate-resilient and beneficial infrastructure projects is a key component of climate finance for economies at all levels of development. Infrastructure finance faces various well-known

Figure 2.7. Sustainability-Linked Bonds—Conceptually Solid Instruments with Practical Issues

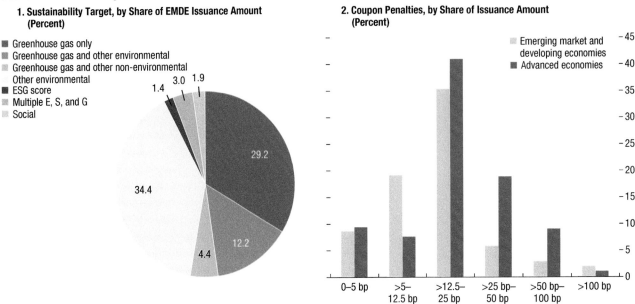

Most sustainability-linked bonds have either a greenhouse gas or another environmental target ...

... but the small penalties are unlikely to be high enough to create strong-enough incentives for issuers to fulfill the pre-agreed target.

1. Sustainability Target, by Share of EMDE Issuance Amount
(Percent)

- Greenhouse gas only
- Greenhouse gas and other environmental
- Greenhouse gas and other non-environmental
- Other environmental
- ESG score
- Multiple E, S, and G
- Social

2. Coupon Penalties, by Share of Issuance Amount
(Percent)

- Emerging market and developing economies
- Advanced economies

Sources: Bloomberg Finance L.P.; and IMF staff calculations.
Note: bp = basis point; EMDE = emerging market and developing economy; ESG = environmental (E), social (S), and governance (G).

challenges, including a lack of investable projects. Supporting the complex development of infrastructure projects, including through technical assistance, and providing financing constitute the core contributions of MDBs.

Sustainability-linked bonds, the main outcome-based debt instrument to date, have been very popular among emerging market issuers and have the potential to be used even more. These bonds feature a contractually agreed sustainability performance target based on a key performance indicator.[13] Unlike green bonds and other use-of-proceeds instruments, issuers may use the proceeds freely. Emissions and other environmental goals (mainly energy efficiency and water consumption) are the dominant performance indicators among emerging-market-based issuers of sustainability-linked bonds (Figure 2.7, panel 1). These bonds may also be used as a transition financing instrument if a target for reduction of greenhouse gas emissions is in line, say, with a net-zero-emission pathway.

[13]For instance, a sustainability performance target could be a firm's direct (scope 1) and indirect greenhouse gas emissions (scope 2), and the associated key performance indicator could be a specific level that the company pledges to achieve by, say, 2030.

These features can be appealing to emerging market and developing economy issuers. Unlike green bonds, which require firms to engage in projects using highly developed green technologies, sustainability-linked bonds signal an improvement over time, independent of the current level of development.

Apart from operational advantages for emerging market issuers, outcome-based instruments can signal to investors that the issuing firm is committed, for example, to improving its emissions over time. The financial incentive to reach the target, if set sufficiently high, can be a strong incentive for the issuer and alleviate investors' concerns about greenwashing. Sustainability-linked bonds, and other outcome-based instruments, are also very suitable for investors looking to ensure the sustainability impact of their investments.

Current practical challenges for sustainability-linked bonds remain. While sustainability targets are sometimes seen to lack ambition (ING 2021), the penalty for not reaching them is often low—in the case of sustainability-linked bonds, less than 25 basis points for most emerging market issuance (Figure 2.7, panel 2). Typically, the penalty comes in the form of a step-up the issuers must pay on the bonds' coupon payments if the sustainability performance target is missed.[14] The penalty event date typically occurs several years after issuance to give the issuer time to reach the performance target. This further reduces the dollar value of the penalty and the incentive for the firm to reach the target.

A new instrument is known as "pay-for-success" finance for climate purposes, also dubbed "environmental impact bonds." While pay-for-success instruments were developed for social projects (social impact bonds), they could also be applied to environmental projects.[15] An important potential use is for adaptation finance. Private sector participation could be particularly effective for adopting less proven but innovative green technologies, where the public sector lacks the necessary expertise. In less developed economies, where capacity to develop such projects is often limited, this financing mechanism could expand the types of potential green and adaptation projects, with the public sector ultimately retaining ownership of the project. It could also incentivize efficient implementation of complex projects if payments to private investors are designed to increase sufficiently with performance. The contractual arrangements are bespoke and complex, however, and require technical assistance as well as assurance against political risks—a potential role for MDBs.

The Role of the IMF and the New Resilience and Sustainability Trust

The IMF can play a catalytic role in climate finance through its policy advice, surveillance, and capacity development by drawing on its track record as a catalyst for official and private finance. The IMF can mitigate macroeconomic risk by providing advice through bilateral and multilateral surveillance, assessing countries' economic and financial developments during Article IV consultations, performing

risk assessments in Financial Sector Assessment Programs, providing climate macro-financial country assessments, and enhancing countries' capacity development. The IMF is already playing a leading part in advocating for carbon pricing. Its Climate-Public Investment Management Assessment is a framework that helps governments identify potential improvements in public investment institutions and processes to build low-carbon and climate-resilient infrastructure (IMF 2021a). This can help give higher priority to climate change mitigation and adaptation in infrastructure development.

Together with other large global policy institutions, the IMF can help strengthen the climate information architecture in emerging market and developing economies. The IMF is playing a key role identifying data gaps, promoting corporate climate-related disclosure, and developing a guidance for taxonomies to ensure interoperability (IMF, Bank for International Settlements, Organisation for Economic Co-operation and Development, and World Bank, forthcoming). Global policy institutions such as the IMF can partner with global data providers to supply them with regularly updated macroeconomic and climate-related data and make such data accessible to the public in a well-structured and accessible way. The IMF has started publishing a Climate Change Indicators Dashboard, which includes indicators on climate financing.[16]

Countries, particularly eligible and qualifying emerging market and developing economies, with limited fiscal space can benefit from IMF Resilience and Sustainability Trust (RST) financing. This new financing facility focuses on longer-term structural changes, including climate change and pandemic preparedness, that entail macroeconomic risk and on policy solutions that have a strong global public good nature (IMF 2022). The RST could play a catalytic role by helping develop a conducive investment climate through reforms that improve the regulatory environment and enhance the quality of data and disclosures, as well as support policies to make infrastructure more resilient.

---

[14]The large majority of sustainability-linked bonds features a coupon step-up (or penalty) in case the sustainability target is missed. In relatively rare cases, the coupon is reduced if the target is reached. The incentive mechanism, however, is symmetric to the case of a coupon penalty (Berrada and others 2022). Other relatively uncommon types of penalties include a redemption premium or a penalty payment to a third party such as a not-for-profit organization dedicated to combating climate change.

[15]To date, environmental impact bonds have been structured only for US municipal projects. The first was issued by DC Water in September 2016 to finance the construction of green infrastructure to manage stormwater runoff in Washington, DC.

[16]The IMF Climate Change Indicators Dashboard includes a range of distinctive indicators that demonstrate the impact of economic activity on climate change, grouped into five categories: economic activity, cross-border, financial and risks, government policy, and climate change data. See https://climatedata.imf.org/.

Figure 2.8. Sovereign Sustainable Debt Issuance

Sovereigns have been latecomers in sustainable debt markets ...

... but usually have had a positive impact on private issuance.

1. Lag between First Corporate Sustainable Bond Issuance and Sovereign Sustainable Bond Issuance
(Months)

2. Annualized Average Corporate Sustainable Bond Issuance before and after First Sovereign Sustainable Bond Issuance
(Percent of GDP)

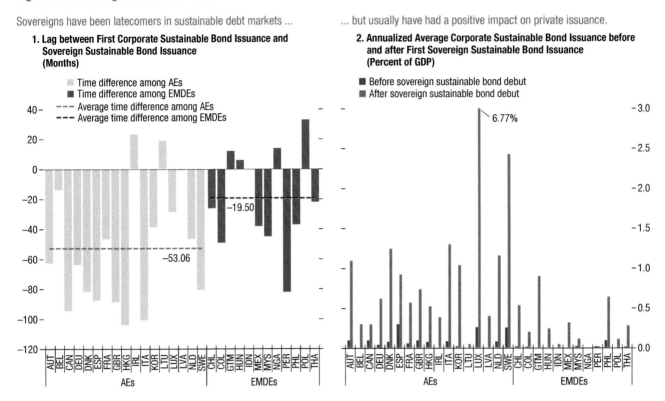

Sources: Bloomberg Finance L.P.; IMF, World Economic Outlook database; and IMF staff calculations.
Note: The data sample includes sustainable bond issuance between 2007 (the issuance of the first sustainable bond) and the end of June 2022. Panel 2 displays annualized average corporate sustainable bond issuance as a percent of GDP. Panels 1 and 2 include only countries where both the government and at least one private firm issued a sustainable bond. Nine countries have issued a sovereign sustainable bond but have not seen private sector issuance. The negative numbers in panel 1 imply that the first corporate sustainable bonds were issued earlier than the first sovereign sustainable bonds. Panels use International Organization for Standardization (ISO) country codes. AE = advanced economy; EMDE = emerging market and developing economy.

Transition Taxonomies

Transition taxonomies, such as those developed in Southeast Asia and discussed earlier in this chapter, can yield significant benefits for emerging market and developing economies. These taxonomies can focus on innovative technologies for sectors in which it is difficult to abate emissions because of technological and cost challenges (such as for cement, steel, chemicals, and heavy-duty transport). They also help promote corporate and financial institutions' disclosure of transition plans to meet the Paris Agreement goals and can inform temperature ratings at the company and portfolio levels. By not relegating carbon-intensive industries—those with the greatest potential to reduce greenhouse gas emissions—to the sidelines, transition taxonomies can be an important tool for emerging market

and developing economies and incentivize private investment informed by climate change targets (see Online Annex 2.3).

The Role of Sovereign Bond Issuance

Sovereign issuers have been latecomers to the issuance of sustainable debt, but they can still have a positive effect on private markets. In most cases, sovereigns issued their first sustainable debt instrument after the private sector did so (Figure 2.8, panel 1). Emerging market and developing economy sovereigns have generally been faster to follow the private sector. The time lag of sovereign sustainable bond issuance has been less than 2 years on average for emerging market and developing economies versus close to 4.5 years for advanced economies. Typically, sovereign issuance has had a positive impact on private issuance, emphasizing the impetus to market development that a sovereign can provide (see Online Annex 2.8 for a formal regression analysis controlling for the momentum in the growth of private debt).[17] In addition, sovereigns can help set sustainability reporting standards. All 39 sovereign issuers to date have detailed issuance frameworks setting high standards. For green bonds, for instance, all sovereign green bond issuance frameworks require at least one second-party opinion (which certifies the use of proceeds for green projects) and impact reports (which document the environmental impact).

The Potential Benefits of the New International Carbon Markets for Emerging Market and Developing Economies

Carbon markets offer substantial opportunities for emerging market and developing economies. The 2021 United Nations Climate Change Conference, known as COP26, has led to completion of the rulebook for implementation of Article 6 of the Paris Agreement, providing a framework to issue carbon credits in a new international carbon market, as well as to trade internationally transferred mitigation outcomes (ITMOs).[18] Advanced economies should be able to buy ITMOs from emerging market and developing economies, opening up a wider market for trade and potentially increasing competition for emission reductions by these economies. Estimates show the potential to generate $330 billion to $475 billion in net financial flows to emerging market and developing economies by 2030 and to prevent up to 6 percent of these economies' total energy-related emissions over the same period (IEA 2021a). Since the COP26, countries have initiated engagement strategies and processes to become potential ITMO sellers and buyers.

---

[17]Nine sovereigns (not shown in Figure 2.8) have issued a sustainable bond that has not been followed by any private issuance from firms in the same jurisdiction. The countries and months of issuance are Andorra (May 2021), Benin (July 2021), Ecuador (January 2020), Egypt (October 2020), Fiji (November 2017), Isle of Man (September 2021), Serbia (September 2021), Slovenia (July 2021), and Uzbekistan (July 2021).

[18]Under Article 6.2 of the Paris Agreement, a country that is achieving its climate objectives faster than it has pledged to in its nationally determined contribution can transfer ITMOs to countries with slower progress. This allows countries with a broad spectrum of mitigation options available to focus on implementing the lowest-cost abatement measures to meet their climate pledges while selling the more expensive emission reductions to international buyers, thereby financing part or all of their climate action.

Despite the opportunities ITMOs present, there are challenges. They offer limited potential for adaptation purposes and make it difficult to avoid double counting of emission reductions by the buyer and seller of ITMOs. In addition, they can be complicated when it comes to cost-efficient implementation of measurement, reporting, and verification processes.

Conclusion and Policy Implications

Scaling up private climate finance in emerging market and developing economies calls for a multipronged approach with improvements across various dimensions, including support from multilateral development banks (MDBs), the IMF, and the public sector. This reflects both the scale of financing needs and the variety of investments needed to achieve material climate change mitigation and adaptation.

Innovative financing instruments can help overcome some of the challenges faced by the private sector in emerging market and developing economies, such as credit and political risks and lack of scale. In larger emerging markets with functioning bond markets, investment funds (such as the Amundi green bond fund set up with the help of the World Bank Group's IFC) provide a good example of how to draw in institutional investors. Such funds should be replicated and scaled up to incentivize issuers in emerging markets to generate a sufficient supply of green assets to finance green projects. By relying on public markets, these funds can draw in large amounts of private finance with relatively little use of MDB or public sector resources.

New types of outcome-based debt instruments—in particular, sustainability-linked bonds—can help alleviate greenwashing if contractual details of these bonds are set properly. For these bonds to achieve a material climate impact, sustainability targets should be linked to emission-reduction targets in line with the Paris Agreement. This type of instrument would be very suitable for emerging market firms with ample scope to improve their emission intensity. The penalties associated with missing the target, however, need to be set such that private issuers have a sufficient incentive to fulfill the targets.

A set of initiatives focused on bolstering the issuance of sustainable bonds by the private sector, local governments, and government agencies should be considered. If small and medium-sized firms do not have access to the bond market, they may not be able to benefit from the initiatives that involve structures with risk-mitigating features at their core. However, MDBs and international financial institutions will remain at the center of initiatives that channel climate funds to emerging market and developing economies by (1) undertaking long-term initiatives to build local currency bond markets to create and promote the development of efficient, scalable, and sound markets; (2) providing guarantees, subsidizing issuance costs, and taking first-loss positions in funding vehicles and securitizations; and (3) assisting in the issuance of climate bonds via technical assistance that improves governments' institutional capacity.

For less developed economies, green infrastructure projects will remain a key instrument, and MDBs will naturally play a key and long-standing role in developing such projects. More climate financing resources could be channeled through MDBs to support such projects by increasing their capital base and reconsidering their approaches to risk appetite via partnerships with the private sector supported by governance and management oversight. MDBs could then make greater use of equity finance (currently only about 1.8 percent of their commitments to climate finance in emerging market and developing economies). MDBs' equity can draw in much larger amounts of private finance, which currently is equal to only about 1.2 times MDBs' own resources.[19] This would likely require governments to increase MDB resources. The costs of increasing funding for MDBs would be more than offset by domestic economic benefits as a result of avoided costs of eventually worthless fossil fuel assets and by the benefits from reduced emissions.

The IMF can play a key role in strengthening the climate information architecture and helping emerging market and developing economies set up climate and other policies to promote private climate finance. Capacity building (along the lines of Article 6.8 of the Paris Agreement) will be paramount to foster the climate information architecture. Ensuring internationally interoperable sustainable finance taxonomies and climate disclosures is essential to avoid fragmentation. Together with other international bodies, the IMF can play an important coordination and facilitation role. Continued advocacy and assistance with the design

and implementation of carbon pricing will remain central: well-calibrated carbon prices can redirect private finance from polluting to "greener" investments.

The IMF's new Resilience and Sustainability Trust (RST) is a catalytic tool to attract climate-related private investment. The RST can provide affordable long-term financing to support countries undertaking macro-critical reforms to reduce risks, including those related to climate change. It provides predictability by improving countries' policy frameworks, with a clear timeline. The additional fiscal space made available by the RST could also be used to co-fund official and private-sector-financed climate-related projects. In doing so, the RST could catalyze (official and) private sector investments for climate-related finance.

Shifting the focus of ESG scores toward sustainability impact and ensuring proper ESG fund labeling practices will likely require external intervention by regulators and supervisors—not only at the national level but coordinated across jurisdictions. ESG scores in their current form are not designed to ensure sustainability impact because they are constructed primarily to reflect ESG-related financial risks. In addition, the labeling practices of ESG funds have come under scrutiny because in some cases the ESG focus of the funds' investment strategies may be less than advertised to investors. Regulators and supervisors could consider introducing clearer and more focused classifications and requirements for ESG funds. The classification systems of the European Union and United Kingdom are prime examples because they set clear and ambitious requirements, including for climate impact.

ESG scores are systematically lower for firms in emerging market and developing economies. This feature and others, such as the high positive correlation between firm size and ESG scores, deserve further investigation. Increased transparency and clarification by ESG rating providers would be welcome.

Substantially strengthening the climate information architecture in emerging market and developing economies is a prerequisite for scaling up private climate finance. Data availability, quality, and comparability in climate-policy-relevant sectors (for example, energy, agriculture, and land use) in these economies should be improved, in conjunction with climate-related corporate disclosure regulations. In addition, methodologies to assess funding gaps should be developed promptly, particularly for the infrastructure gap in climate change mitigation and adaptation. Transition taxonomies are

---

[19]A detailed proposal for MDBs to provide equity financing to replace coal with renewables is presented in a recent IMF working paper (Adrian, Bolton, and Kleinnijenhuis 2022).

prime tools to enhance data collection regarding decarbonization options and characteristics in hard-to-abate and carbon-intensive sectors across value chains (see Online Annex 2.3). While such asset-level approaches can inform transition plans at a corporate level, they may also be useful to develop portfolio-level alignment methodologies. They can provide a clear signal by emerging market and developing economy issuers about the climate benefits of their assets, including in sectors with ample scope for emission reductions. Shared common and operationalized principles for such taxonomies and other alignment approaches would avoid fragmentation and misalignment and foster comparability and consistency across jurisdictions while taking into consideration these economies' specific industrial structure, as well as decarbonization and adaptation priorities.

The international carbon market envisioned under Article 6 of the Paris Agreement could foster climate finance in emerging market and developing economies—particularly adaptation finance. The momentum generated by COP26 should be leveraged to fully implement the international carbon market mechanisms, since there is agreement on the key rules and modalities for their implementation. Both implementation of the bilateral trade of carbon

emission reduction among nations (Article 6.2) and global trading of carbon emission reductions (Article 6.4, similar to the Clean Development Mechanism) could significantly reduce the costs of achieving the temperature goals of the Paris Agreement. The global market under Article 6.4 will directly support adaptation finance in emerging market and developing economies by transferring a fixed share of traded carbon to a fund to finance adaptation projects and programs in developing economies (the "Adaptation Fund"). This has the potential to provide a very significant increase in much-needed adaptation finance. Parties to the UNFCCC as well as MDBs should therefore provide as much support as possible toward timely and full implementation of the UNFCCC international carbon markets.

In parallel, specialized public climate funds, such as the Green Climate Fund (also under the auspices of the UNFCCC), should receive sufficient resources to fill the adaptation financing gap. Advanced economies should allocate to such funds a significant share of their annual financing pledges to developing economies under the Paris Agreement. Adaptation finance often cannot generate returns for private investors, but it can yield very large social benefits for the countries most affected by climate change.

References

Adrian, Tobias, Patrick Bolton, and Alissa M. Kleinnijenhuis. 2022. "The Great Carbon Arbitrage." IMF Working Paper 22/107, International Monetary Fund, Washington, DC.

Basu, Priya, Lisa Finneran, Veronique Bishop, and Trichur Sundararaman. 2011. "The Scope for MDB Leverage and Innovation in Climate Finance." World Bank, Washington, DC.

Berg, Florian, Julian F. Kölbel, and Roberto Rigobon. 2022. "Aggregate Confusion: The Divergence of ESG Rating." *Review of Finance* rfac033. https://doi.org/10.1093/rof/rfac033

Berrada, Tony, Leonie Engelhardt, Rajna Gibson, and Philipp Krueger. 2022. "The Economics of Sustainability Linked Bonds." Swiss Finance Institute Research Paper 22–26, Zurich.

Bhattacharya, Amar, Meagan Dooley, Homi Kharas, Charlotte Taylor, and Nicholas Stern. 2022. "Financing a Big Investment Push in Emerging Markets and Developing Economies for Sustainable, Resilient and Inclusive Recovery and Growth." Grantham Research Institute on Climate Change and the Environment, London School of Economics and Political Science, and Brookings Institution, London.

Bolton, Patrick, Xavier Musca, and Frédéric Samama. 2020. "Global Public-Private Investment Partnerships: A Financing Innovation with Positive Social Impact." *Journal of Applied Corporate Finance* 32 (2): 31–41.

Chapagain, Dipesh, Florent Baarsch, Michiel Schaeffer, and Sarah D'haen. 2020. "Climate Change Adaptation Costs in Developing Countries: Insights from Existing Estimates." *Climate and Development* 12 (10): 934–42.

Climate Policy Initiative. 2021. "Global Landscape of Climate Finance 2021."

Drempetic, Samuel, Christian Klein, and Bernhard Zwergel. 2020. "The Influence of Firm Size on the ESG Score: Corporate Sustainability Ratings under Review." *Journal of Business Ethics* 167 (2): 333–60.

Ehlers, Torsten. 2014. "Understanding the Challenges of Infrastructure Finance." BIS Working Paper 454, Bank for International Settlements, Basel.

Elmalt, Dalya, Divya Kirti, and Deniz Igan. 2021. "Limits to Private Climate Change Mitigation." IMF Working Paper 21/112, International Monetary Fund, Washington, DC.

Fouad, Manal, Natalija Novta, Gemma Preston, Todd Schneider, and Sureni Weerathunga. 2021. "Unlocking Access to Climate Finance for Pacific Islands Countries." IMF Departmental Paper 2021/020, International Monetary Fund, Washington, DC.

Global Sustainable Investment Alliance (GSIA). 2020. *Global Sustainable Investment Review 2020*. Sydney.

ING Group (ING). 2021. "The Credibility of the Sustainability-linked Loan and Bond Markets." Position paper, Amsterdam.

International Energy Agency (IEA). 2021a. "Financing Clean Energy Transitions in Emerging and Developing Economies." World Energy Investment 2021 Special Report, Paris.

International Energy Agency (IEA). 2021b. *Global Energy Review 2021*. Paris.

International Monetary Fund (IMF). 2021a. "Strengthening Infrastructure Governance for Climate-Responsive Public Investment." IMF Policy Paper, Washington, DC.

International Monetary Fund (IMF). 2021b. "Strengthening the Climate Information Architecture." Staff Climate Note 2021/003, Washington, DC.

International Monetary Fund (IMF). 2022. "Proposal to Establish a Resilience and Sustainability Trust." IMF Policy Paper, Washington, DC.

International Monetary Fund (IMF), Bank for International Settlements (BIS), Organisation for Economic Co-operation and Development (OECD), and World Bank (WB). Forthcoming. "Operationalization of the Principles for Sustainable Finance Alignment Approaches."

Network for Greening the Financial System (NGFS). 2022a. "Central Banking and Supervision in the Biosphere: An Agenda for Action on Biodiversity Loss, Financial Risk and System Stability." Paris.

Network for Greening the Financial System (NGFS). 2022b. "Final Report on Bridging Data Gaps." Paris.

Prasad, Ananthakrishnan, Elena Loukoianova, Alan Xiaochen Feng, and William Oman. 2022. "Mobilizing Private Climate Financing in Emerging Market and Developing Economies." IMF Staff Climate Note 2022/007, International Monetary Fund, Washington, DC.

United Nations Environment Programme (UNEP). 2021. "Adaptation Gap Report 2021: The Gathering Storm—Adapting to Climate Change in a Post-Pandemic World." Nairobi.

World Bank. 2019. "Beyond the Gap: How Countries Can Afford the Infrastructure They Need while Protecting the Planet." World Bank Sustainable Infrastructure Series, Washington, DC.

ASSET PRICE FRAGILITY IN TIMES OF STRESS: THE ROLE OF OPEN-END INVESTMENT FUNDS

Chapter 3 at a Glance

- Since the global financial crisis, there has been remarkable growth in open-end investment funds. The total value of their net assets has quadrupled since 2008, reaching $41 trillion in the first quarter of 2022 and accounting for approximately one-fifth of the assets of the nonbank financial sector.
- Open-end funds play an important role in financial markets, but those that offer daily redemptions while holding illiquid assets can amplify the effects of adverse shocks by raising the likelihood of investor runs and asset fire sales. This contributes to volatility in asset markets and potentially threatens financial stability.
- These concerns are particularly pertinent now as central banks normalize policy amid heightened uncertainty about the outlook. A disorderly tightening of financial conditions could trigger significant redemptions from these funds and contribute to stress in asset markets.
- Assets (particularly bonds) held by relatively illiquid funds are more "fragile," with higher return volatility, especially in periods of market stress. A significant decline in fund liquidity such as that observed during the March 2020 market turmoil can increase bond return volatility by more than 20 percent.
- Investments by advanced economy open-end funds in emerging markets have grown significantly over the past decade, with important implications. A significant decline in the liquidity of advanced economy bond funds comparable to that observed in March 2020 can increase the return volatility of emerging market corporate bonds by more than 20 percent.
- Importantly, the adverse effects of less liquid open-end investment funds on asset prices could lead to a tightening of domestic financial conditions, reinforcing the vicious cycle between investor runs and asset market volatility.

Policy recommendations

- Policymakers should ensure that adequate liquidity management tools are used by these funds. A wide range of tools is available to potentially mitigate the vulnerabilities and systemic impact of open-end funds, but effective implementation of these tools is lacking.
- Tools that aim to limit vulnerabilities by reducing the risk of investor runs, such as swing pricing or antidilution levies, can be potentially effective to mitigate asset price fragilities associated with less liquid open-end funds. Swing pricing is routinely used by open-end funds in some jurisdictions, but to further strengthen its effectiveness, policymakers should provide guidance on its implementation, ensure that swing factors fully reflect the price impact of trades, and encourage disclosure of swing pricing practices and calibration methodologies.
- Additional liquidity management tools could include limiting the frequency of redemptions by linking it to the liquidity of funds' portfolios to directly address the underlying vulnerability related to the liquidity mismatch.
- Tighter monitoring of funds' liquidity risk management practices by supervisors and regulators should be considered.
- Given the adverse cross-border spillover effects, recipient economies need to take appropriate policy responses to mitigate potential systemic risks from volatile capital flows sourced from open-end funds. These should include continued deepening of domestic markets; the use of macroeconomic, prudential, and capital flow management measures; and foreign exchange intervention in line with the recommendations of the International Monetary Fund's Institutional View.[1]

The authors of this chapter are Andrea Deghi, Zhi Ken Gan, Pierre Guérin, Anna-Theresa Helmke, Tara Iyer, Junghwan Mok, Xinyi Su, and Felix Suntheim (lead) under the guidance of Fabio Natalucci, Mahvash Qureshi, and Mario Catalán. Itay Goldstein served as an expert advisor.

[1]For additional information, see https://www.imf.org/en/Publications/Policy-Papers/Issues/2022/03/29/Review-of-The-Institutional-View-on-The-Liberalization-and-Management-of-Capital-Flows-515883.

Introduction

The rapid growth of open-end investment funds (OEFs) has raised concerns about financial stability. OEFs, which are mutual funds that can issue or redeem shares daily at a price set at the end of the trading day, are an important component of the nonbank financial sector and have grown significantly in the past two decades.[2] Their total net assets have quadrupled since the global financial crisis, reaching $41 trillion in the first quarter of 2022 and accounting for approximately one-fifth of the nonbank financial sector's assets (Figure 3.1, panel 1). The growth of the OEF sector reflects the increasing shift in financial intermediation from banks to nonbank financial institutions, which can be attributed at least in part to the tighter regulations on banks as well as bank balance sheet deleveraging following the global financial crisis (see the April 2015 *Global Financial Stability Report* [GFSR]).[3] Most OEFs are domiciled in advanced economies and invest in equities issued in advanced economies (Figure 3.1, panel 2); however, the share of funds investing in relatively less liquid assets, such as corporate bonds or emerging market bonds and equities, has been rising rapidly (Figure 3.1, panel 3).[4] The growing importance of OEFs for the functioning and liquidity of asset markets has prompted increased scrutiny of their potential role in amplifying excessive volatility—or "fragility"—in these markets, especially when market liquidity deteriorates.[5]

OEFs holding illiquid assets can worsen fragility in asset markets through the liquidity mismatch between their asset holdings and liabilities. In the face of adverse shocks, OEFs that offer daily redemptions to investors but hold relatively less liquid assets are vulnerable to the risk of investor runs (or large outflows) that could force these funds to sell assets to meet redemptions. The sale of assets could in turn generate downward pressure on asset prices that may amplify the initial effects of the shocks by inducing additional redemptions. These price pressures would be further intensified if funds were to engage in herding—that is, mimic other investors' trading behavior, possibly ignoring their own information and beliefs.[6]

Financial stability concerns about OEFs resurfaced during the financial market turmoil of March 2020. Amid heightened uncertainty about the economic outlook, OEFs that were invested in relatively less liquid assets experienced historic outflows and a "dash for cash" at the onset of the COVID-19 pandemic (Figure 3.2). This contributed to market dislocations and liquidity problems that were resolved only after unprecedented policy responses by major central banks—in particular, the purchase of corporate bonds and exchange-traded funds (ETFs) in primary and secondary markets (Liang 2020; Falato, Goldstein, and Hortaçsu 2021; Hespeler and Suntheim 2020; IMF 2021).

The resilience of the OEF sector may be tested again if financial conditions tighten abruptly as central banks normalize the stance of monetary policy. Amid persistent inflationary pressures, major central banks are significantly normalizing their policy stance, and financial conditions have tightened since the beginning of 2022 (see Chapter 1). This has coincided with large outflows from OEFs in recent months, especially from high-yield corporate bond funds and emerging market equity and bond funds (Figure 3.3). More aggressive monetary policy tightening by central banks against a backdrop of continued inflationary pressure, as well as increased uncertainty about the macroeconomic outlook stemming from persistent supply chain disruptions and

---

[2]The end-of-day net asset value reflects the difference between the total value of the fund's assets and liabilities divided by the number of shares outstanding. OEFs are different from other types of investment funds such as closed-end funds, which issue a fixed number of shares initially to raise capital for investments that can later be traded on secondary markets between investors but not redeemed. They also differ from exchange-traded funds, which can be traded on exchanges throughout the day, similarly to stocks, but whose shares can be created and redeemed only by authorized participants.

[3]These factors may possibly be working in conjunction with an increased demand for financial products offering daily liquidity.

[4]OEFs invest in different types of assets, ranging from very liquid (such as cash or short-term, highly rated sovereign bonds) to less liquid (such as certain types of corporate bonds) to highly illiquid (such as real estate or infrastructure investments). Assets that are liquid can be bought or sold in a short period of time at a low cost (that is, without affecting their price). However, liquidity can vary across assets and over time. The focus of this chapter is primarily on funds investing in bonds and equities, and implications of their relative illiquidity are examined.

[5]Excessive volatility or fragility is induced in asset prices if they are susceptible to trading shocks that sway these prices away from their fundamental values (Greenwood and Thesmar 2011). See the April 2015 GFSR for a detailed discussion of the possible role of investment funds in generating macro-financial stability risks.

[6]Studies show evidence of herding by OEFs, especially when market stress is elevated (for example, Brown, Wei, and Wermers 2014; Cai and others 2019). Leverage is another potential factor that could exacerbate existing vulnerabilities and contribute to asset price fragility. An analysis of fund leverage is outside the scope of this chapter due to data limitations.

Figure 3.1. Developments in Open-End Investment Funds

Open-end investment funds have grown substantially and now represent approximately one-fifth of the nonbank financial sector.

Most of these funds are domiciled in advanced economies ...

... and have been increasingly investing in less liquid assets.

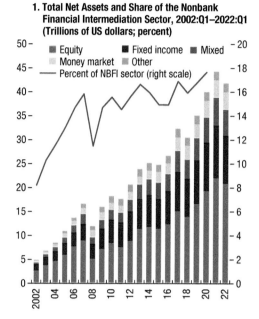

1. Total Net Assets and Share of the Nonbank Financial Intermediation Sector, 2002:Q1–2022:Q1 (Trillions of US dollars; percent)

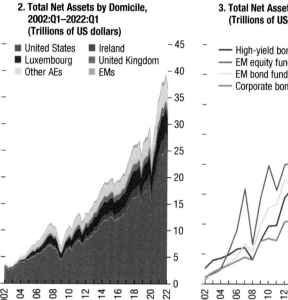

2. Total Net Assets by Domicile, 2002:Q1–2022:Q1 (Trillions of US dollars)

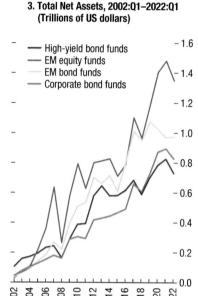

3. Total Net Assets, 2002:Q1–2022:Q1 (Trillions of US dollars)

Sources: Financial Stability Board (2021); Morningstar; and IMF staff calculations.
Note: In panel 1, NBFI includes all financial institutions that are not central banks, banks, or public financial institutions (Financial Stability Board 2022). Panel 3 shows groupings based on Morningstar classifications; groupings may overlap and are not mutually exclusive. EM bond funds include both corporate bond funds and sovereign bond funds. Total net asset value is the difference between the total value of a fund's assets and liabilities. AE = advanced economy; EM = emerging market; NBFI = nonbank financial intermediation.

Russia's invasion of Ukraine (see Chapter 1 of the October 2022 *World Economic Outlook*) could cause a sudden repricing of risk and a disorderly tightening of global financial conditions. Such an adverse shock, combined with the inherent vulnerability of OEFs holding illiquid assets but offering daily redemptions, could trigger further outflows from these funds and amplify stress in asset markets.

An adverse shock to the OEF sector could have significant ramifications for emerging market economies. Since the global financial crisis, these economies have received large capital inflows from OEFs, especially into bond markets (Figure 3.4). At the onset of the pandemic in March 2020, emerging market economies saw large and abrupt outflows of about $78 billion, followed by sustained and large inflows. More recently, in the face of tighter global financial conditions, investors have retrenched from emerging market economies, with outflows from equity and bond markets totaling $69 billion since the beginning of 2022. A disorderly

tightening in global financial conditions could trigger further fund outflows and a worsening of financial conditions in these economies.[7]

Despite the financial stability risks, effective implementation of policy measures by governments or regulatory authorities to mitigate the vulnerabilities associated with OEFs holding illiquid assets has been lacking. Several policy options are available to address these vulnerabilities and risks through better liquidity management by funds. Liquidity management tools could be applied to the asset side of funds' balance sheets (for example, limits on investing in illiquid assets or limits on asset concentration and requirements to hold a minimum amount of liquid assets).

[7]In the case of emerging markets, the importance of benchmark-driven portfolio flows has increased significantly over the years, which poses additional risk as these flows tend to be highly sensitive to global factors, potentially increasing the risk of excessive outflows with a spike in investor risk aversion (Arslanalp and others 2020; April 2019 *Global Financial Stability Report* [GFSR]).

Figure 3.2. How the March 2020 Market Turmoil Highlighted the Vulnerabilities of Open-End Investment Funds

In March 2020, open-end investment funds experienced larger outflows than in previous market stress episodes ...

... especially from relatively less liquid funds such as high-yield bond funds.

1. **Monthly Net Flows, 2002:Q1–2022:Q1**
   (Percent of lagged total net assets)

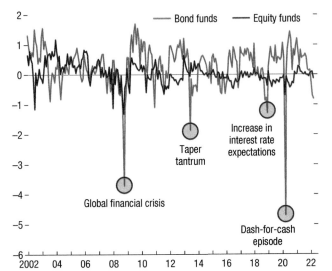

2. **Monthly Net Flows of High-Yield and Investment-Grade Bond Funds, 2002:Q1–2022:Q1**
   (Percent of lagged total net assets)

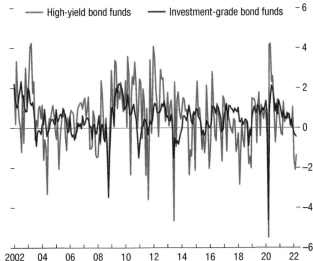

Sources: Morningstar; and IMF staff calculations.
Note: Panel 2 shows fund groupings based on Morningstar classifications.

Figure 3.3. Large Outflows from Open-End Investment Funds amid Monetary Policy Tightening by Major Central Banks

In recent months, outflows from open-end bond funds have increased sharply in sync with the tightening of monetary policy by the Federal Reserve.

Outflows have also been pronounced from emerging market bond and equity funds.

1. **Cumulative Fund Flows into Open-End Bond Funds and Federal Funds Rate, July 2021–July 2022**
   (Percent)

2. **Cumulative Fund Flows into Emerging Market Open-End Investment Funds and Federal Funds Rate, July 2021–July 2022**
   (Percent)

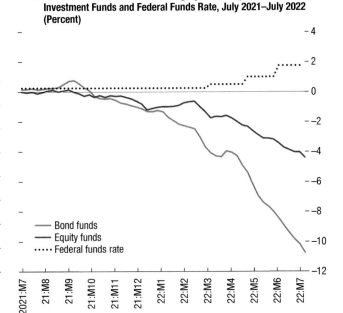

Sources: Emerging Portfolio Fund Research; and IMF staff calculations.
Note: Cumulative flows are calculated based on US dollar flows as a percent of beginning of period's total net asset values.

Figure 3.4. Cross-Border Investment by Open-End Investment Funds in Emerging Market Economies

Open-end investment funds have been playing an increasingly important role in emerging markets ...

... and especially in bond markets.

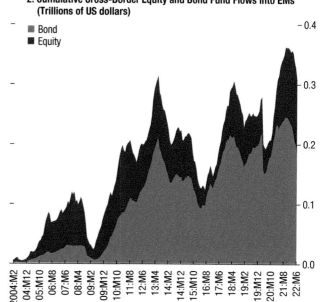

1. Funds' Portfolio Allocations into EM Bond and Equity Markets (Trillions of US dollars)

- Emerging Asia
- Emerging Europe
- Latin America
- Middle East
- Africa

2. Cumulative Cross-Border Equity and Bond Fund Flows into EMs (Trillions of US dollars)

- Bond
- Equity

Sources: Emerging Portfolio Fund Research; and IMF staff calculations.
Note: EM = emerging market.

They could also be applied to the liability side (such as in-kind redemptions, redemption suspensions or gates, and side pockets, as well as price-based measures such as redemption fees, antidilution levies, and "swing pricing").[8]

Studies point to the potential effectiveness of price-based measures such as swing pricing, redemption fees, and antidilution levies in reducing investors' incentive to run on funds.[9] These measures ensure that trading costs are borne only by the exiting investors, for example, by adjusting the net asset value when facing outflows (swing pricing) or by imposing a fee on redeeming investors (antidilution levies). This is desirable from an investor protection perspective—both in normal times and in times of market stress—because it prevents dilution of the shares of the fund's remaining investors. But it also has a systemic impact by dampening investors' incentive to redeem ahead of others, thereby reducing the risk of investor runs. Moreover, unlike other tools, such as less frequent redemptions (or "gates"), price-based measures do not restrict funds' ability to provide daily liquidity—which is a key feature of OEFs. However, to date, these measures have been adopted only by funds in certain jurisdictions, and there are questions about their calibration and effectiveness, especially in periods of severe market stress (Lewrick and others 2022).

In the absence of adequate liquidity management by funds, central banks have stepped in during episodes of severe market stress to provide liquidity backstops to the financial sector, including to OEFs, but such interventions may lead to underpricing of risk

[8]In-kind redemptions are a tool by which a fund's portfolio assets are distributed to redeeming investors on a pro rata basis. Suspensions temporarily prevent investors from withdrawing their capital from a fund. Redemption gates restrict investors' ability to redeem when total redemptions exceed a certain level. Side pockets are subfunds (segregated accounts) that typically hold less liquid assets and have longer redemption periods. Redemption fees are charges imposed on investors redeeming their shares, typically to discourage short-term trading. Antidilution levies are fees imposed on redeeming investors to compensate the remaining investors for the transaction costs caused by the redemptions. Swing pricing allows funds to adjust their net asset value based on the transactions of the redeeming investors such that trading costs are borne by the exiting investors.

[9]See, for example, Jin and others (2022) and Emter, Fecht, and Peia (2022).

by investors. Unlike banks, investment funds do not generally have access to central bank liquidity facilities or deposit insurance. They are also not subject to the same intensity of prudential oversight, or to the capital and liquidity requirements, imposed on banks. However, in episodes of severe market stress, such as during the March 2020 market turmoil, central banks have had to purchase a range of risky assets, including corporate bonds, to ease strains on liquidity to help prevent asset fire sales by funds, which could have led to a further deterioration in market liquidity. Such interventions, while at times warranted to prevent systemic crises, may result in moral hazard and systematic underpricing of risk by funds.[10] It is therefore essential to work toward a policy and regulatory framework that addresses the vulnerabilities associated with OEFs, and mitigates potential risks to financial stability, while minimizing the need for central banks to intervene in financial markets.

Against this backdrop, this chapter analyzes the contribution of OEFs to asset price fragility and discusses different policy options to mitigate the risks. The chapter begins by laying out a simple conceptual framework to discuss the nature of potential financial stability risks arising from OEFs. Next, it uses a sample of 17,000 OEFs domiciled in 43 countries and holding more than 450,000 bond and equity securities and examines a period from the fourth quarter of 2013 to the second quarter of 2022 to construct quantitative measures of vulnerabilities of OEFs, defined mainly in terms of the illiquidity of their asset holdings.[11] The chapter then empirically analyzes the extent to which these vulnerabilities drive fragility in asset markets—measured as volatility of asset returns—especially during episodes of market stress. It also examines potential cross-border spillovers from funds domiciled in advanced economies to asset prices in emerging market economies. In addition, it investigates the channels through which fund illiquidity

is transmitted to asset price fragility and assesses its impact on broader financial conditions. Finally, the chapter analyzes the role of liquidity risk management tools in mitigating the vulnerabilities and risks associated with OEFs.[12]

A Conceptual Framework to Understand the Financial Stability Risks of Open-End Investment Funds

OEFs that hold illiquid assets but offer daily redemptions to investors may experience severe outflows in periods of market stress. OEFs that offer such daily redemptions but hold assets that cannot be liquidated quickly without material loss of value are subject to an asset-liability "liquidity" mismatch. This mismatch reflects an inherent vulnerability of the fund that gives rise to the risk of sudden and large redemptions by investors (runs on funds). The risk arises because investors can redeem shares from the fund on a daily basis at its current net asset value without bearing the full transaction costs of their redemptions. These costs are then effectively borne by the investors who remain in the fund.[13] This externality creates an incentive for investors to redeem ahead of others—known as the "first-mover advantage"—particularly from funds that hold less liquid assets that may be more difficult and costly to sell (Chen, Goldstein, and Jiang 2010; Goldstein, Jiang, and Ng 2017).

Funds facing outflows may be forced to sell assets, putting downward pressure on asset prices. In the face of redemptions, OEFs may need to sell assets to pay out investors if the funds do not have enough cash or cash-like assets. This could depress asset prices, particularly of less liquid assets, amid tight

---

[10]Moral hazard could arise because repeated liquidity support by central banks may incentivize funds as well as end investors to take on more risk without fully internalizing the costs of such risk-taking.

[11]The sample period is chosen based on the availability of consistent portfolio holdings data required for the empirical analysis. See Online Annex 3.1 for a detailed description of the sample and variable definitions. All online annexes are available at www.imf.org/en/Publications/GFSR.

[12]Several studies have assessed the role of funds in generating fragility in corporate bond and equity markets. The main contribution of this chapter is to use a global sample of funds, composed of both equity and bond funds, investing in a large group of advanced and emerging market economies. In addition, the chapter looks at the transmission of shocks from OEFs to broader financial conditions, examines the cross-border spillover effects of fund vulnerabilities on asset prices and financial conditions, compares OEFs with ETFs, and analyzes several policy options.

[13]Transaction costs include direct costs such as commissions and fees, as well as indirect costs such as the impact on asset prices resulting from their sale by the fund to meet redemption requests. The price impact tends to be larger when the underlying market liquidity is poor.

Figure 3.5. Liquidity Mismatch of Open-End Investment Funds and Systemic Risk

Redemptions from open-end funds can trigger fire sales of assets that can result in tighter overall financial conditions.

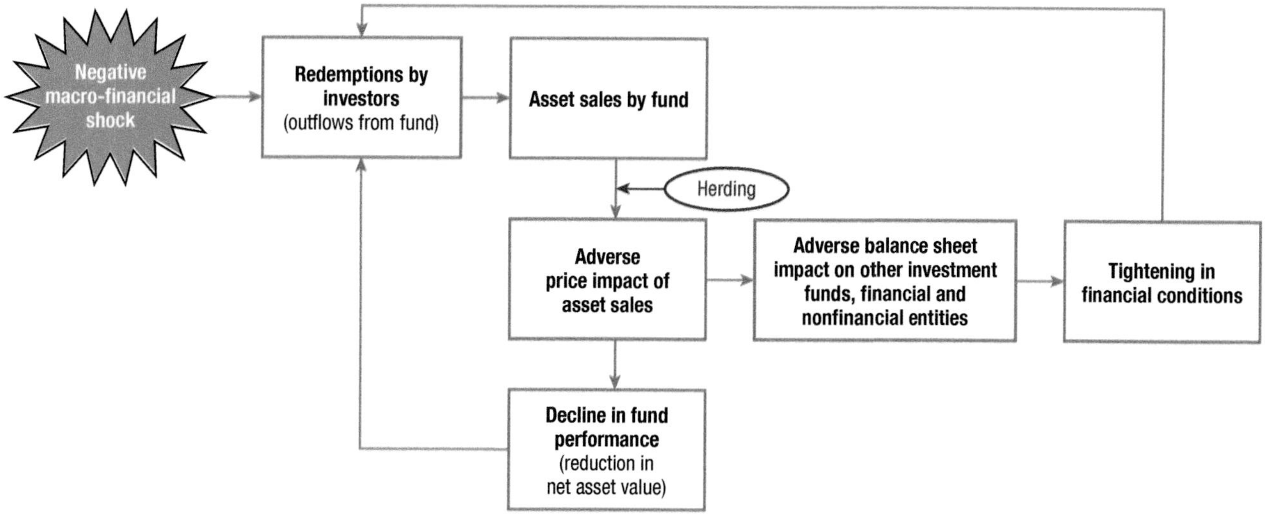

Source: Prepared by IMF staff.
Note: In addition to the adverse price impact, asset sales by the fund can incur other transaction costs such as commissions and fees, which will adversely affect its net asset value. High leverage and low levels of liquidity provision in the market could further amplify the impact of redemptions on asset sales.

financial conditions (Figure 3.5).[14] Moreover, in the presence of herding by funds, trading activity in the same direction could exacerbate selling pressure and cause asset prices to diverge from fundamental values.

Depressed asset values can, in turn, lower the performance of funds and induce further redemptions and asset fire sales, amplifying the impact of shocks. Lower asset prices could also adversely affect the balance sheets of other financial and nonfinancial entities, including funds not originally affected by the shock, and potentially lead to a broad-based tightening

of financial conditions that could reinforce the vicious cycle of redemptions and asset fire sales, thus threatening macro-financial stability.[15]

Vulnerabilities of Open-End Investment Funds and Asset Markets: Some Stylized Facts

OEFs that invest in corporate bonds, especially high-yield bonds, tend to be much more illiquid than equity funds. Because the first-mover advantage for investors will generally be greater in less liquid funds, the level of illiquidity of a fund's portfolio is a useful gauge of its vulnerability. Illiquidity is measured here as the value-weighted average of the bid-ask spreads of the securities held by the fund.[16] By that measure, illiquidity tends to be much higher for bond funds than for equity funds (Figure 3.6, panel 1). Among bond funds,

---

[14]Jiang and others (2022) find that redemptions from corporate bond funds generate price pressures and that during the COVID-19 crisis bonds held largely by more illiquid funds experienced more negative returns. By contrast, Choi and others (2020) find little evidence for such price pressures after controlling for issuer-time fixed effects, which they attribute to funds' liquidity management strategies. Ma, Xiao, and Zeng (2022) reconcile the findings by showing that the price impact generated by the unprecedented outflows during the COVID-19 pandemic depended on the pecking order of liquidation adopted by funds. In periods of stress, price pressures can emerge even in otherwise liquid assets. In equity markets, Coval and Stafford (2007) show, outflows from mutual funds put price pressure on securities that are sold by distressed funds.

[15]Depressed asset prices can also adversely affect the ability of firms to raise capital (Zhu 2021).

[16]Bid-ask spreads are a widely used measure of liquidity that reflect the difference between "sell" and "buy" prices quoted by market participants, such as broker dealers. Alternative measures rely on higher-frequency price data or transaction data, which are not available for the global sample and various asset classes considered in this chapter.

Figure 3.6. Liquidity of the Portfolio Holdings of Open-End Investment Funds

The liquidity of funds' portfolios has generally been stable but deteriorated dramatically in March 2020 ...

... particularly for high-yield and EM bond funds.

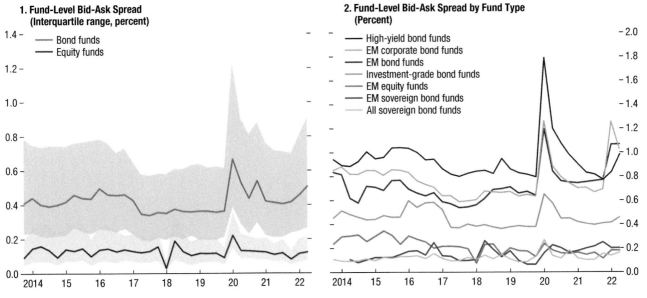

Sources: FactSet; Morningstar; Refinitiv; and IMF staff calculations.
Note: Fund-level illiquidity is the weighted average of the bid-ask spreads of the fund's portfolio of securities. In panel 1, the solid lines indicate the median, and the shaded area indicates the interquartile range of fund-level illiquidity. In panel 2, the median fund-level bid-ask spreads are shown for groupings of assets based on Morningstar classifications; these groupings are not mutually exclusive. EM = emerging market.

those holding corporate high-yield bonds and emerging market bonds tend to be the most illiquid, while those investing in sovereign bonds are the most liquid (Figure 3.6, panel 2).

The liquidity of funds' portfolios deteriorated dramatically during the March 2020 market turmoil and has been worsening again in recent months. The liquidity of OEF portfolios had been relatively stable for several years before the COVID-19 pandemic but deteriorated rapidly in March 2020 amid heightened uncertainty about the outlook. The deterioration in fund-level liquidity, indicated by the increase in bid-ask spreads of funds' portfolios, was particularly severe for funds invested in relatively less liquid assets, such as high-yield and emerging market bonds. Consistent with the view that liquidity mismatches heighten the risk of runs on funds, redemptions from these funds reached record levels, as shown in Figure 3.2. The liquidity of funds' portfolios worsened again in the first half of 2022, especially for high-yield and emerging market bond funds. In fact, for the latter, liquidity reached levels similar to that observed in March 2020 (Figure 3.6).

Assets held by more illiquid funds may be more susceptible to selling pressure caused by large redemptions from funds. To gauge the extent to which assets are vulnerable to selling pressure stemming from fund redemptions, the analysis constructs an asset-level "vulnerability measure" that captures the illiquidity of the portfolios of funds holding that asset.[17] Not surprisingly, the data show that less liquid assets such as bonds are generally held by more illiquid funds and are therefore more vulnerable to selling pressure than equities (Figure 3.7, panel 1). Across different types of bonds, corporate high-yield and emerging market bonds are more likely to be held by more illiquid funds and are hence highly vulnerable to fund redemptions (Figure 3.7, panel 2). The vulnerability of these assets increased dramatically during the COVID-19 crisis, when liquidity mismatches in

---

[17]The measure is constructed following Jiang and others (2022) and captures the weighted-average liquidity of the funds holding the assets, with liquidity defined as the value-weighted quoted bid-ask spread of funds' portfolios and the weights reflecting the share of a fund's ownership of the asset. See Online Annex 3.2 for further details.

Figure 3.7. Asset-Level Vulnerability Measure

Fixed-income securities are held by more illiquid funds and are thus on average more vulnerable than equity securities.

Less liquid securities such as high-yield and EM bonds are generally held by more illiquid funds, and recently their vulnerabilities have reached levels almost as high as in March 2020.

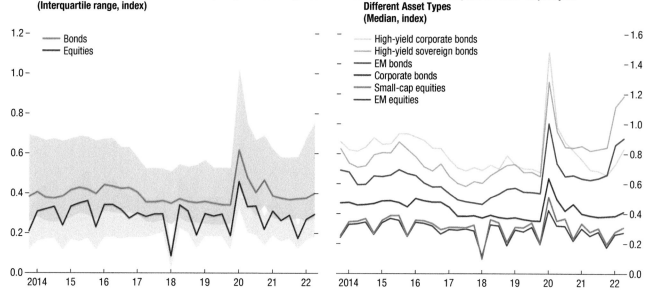

1. Asset-Level Vulnerability due to Funds' Illiquidity: Bonds vs. Equities
(Interquartile range, index)

2. Asset-Level Vulnerability due to Funds' Illiquidity for Different Asset Types
(Median, index)

Sources: FactSet; Morningstar; Refinitiv; and IMF staff calculations.
Note: Panel 1 displays the evolution of asset-level vulnerabilities for bonds and equities. The vulnerability measure is constructed following Jiang and others (2022) and captures the weighted average liquidity of its owners, with liquidity defined as the portfolio-level bid-ask spread. See Online Appendix 3.2 for further details. In panel 1, the solid line indicates the median, and the shaded area is the interquartile range for the asset-level vulnerability measure. In panel 2, the lines indicate the median asset-level vulnerability for specific asset classes. EM = emerging market.

OEFs increased (as shown in Figure 3.6), and it has risen again in 2022, in some cases close to levels seen during the early days of the pandemic.

More vulnerable assets experience sharper price declines than other assets in periods of market stress. The higher vulnerability of assets held by less liquid funds is visible during two recent episodes of market stress. In March 2020, at the height of the financial market turmoil driven by the COVID-19 pandemic, fixed-income securities held by more illiquid funds experienced a sharper drop in prices (that is, lower returns) than those held by liquid funds (Figure 3.8, panel 1). This pattern was repeated in the first half of 2022, when global asset markets declined in response to monetary policy tightening by major central banks and the war in Ukraine (Figure 3.8, panel 2).[18]

[18]For equities, no meaningful difference is found between the returns of those held by more vulnerable funds relative to less vulnerable funds, consistent with the notion that liquidity mismatches play a less important role in more liquid markets such as the equity market.

Taken together, these initial observations suggest that the vulnerabilities of OEFs could indeed adversely affect asset markets. In the discussion that follows, the chapter investigates the strength of the relationship between fund-level vulnerabilities and the fragility in asset markets (measured by the volatility of equity and bond returns).

How Open-End Investment Fund Vulnerabilities Can Contribute to the Fragility of Asset Prices

Individual fixed-income securities that are held by less liquid funds tend to have more volatile returns than those held by liquid funds, after taking into account a wide range of other security characteristics that could affect the volatility of returns. The empirical analysis shows that the illiquidity of OEFs contributes to the fragility of bond returns in addition to what can be expected based on other bond characteristics, including their liquidity, rating, and

Figure 3.8. Bonds Held by Vulnerable Funds Have Underperformed in 2020 and 2022

During the dash-for-cash episode in March 2020, bonds held by more illiquid funds had lower returns.

Vulnerable securities have also underperformed so far in the 2022 bear market.

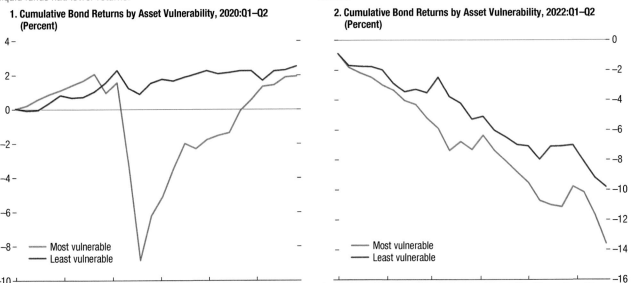

1. Cumulative Bond Returns by Asset Vulnerability, 2020:Q1–Q2
(Percent)

2. Cumulative Bond Returns by Asset Vulnerability, 2022:Q1–Q2
(Percent)

Sources: Morningstar; and IMF staff calculations.

Note: Most (least) vulnerable bonds are those in the top (bottom) tercile of the distribution of the asset-level vulnerability measure in 2019:Q4 (panel 1) and 2021:Q4 (panel 2). Average cumulative returns are weighted by market value. See Online Annex 3.2 for a more comprehensive econometric analysis confirming results in this descriptive analysis.

maturity (Figure 3.9).[19] A one standard deviation increase in the vulnerability measure of an average bond increases its return volatility by 23 percent relative to the median return volatility of the bond (first bar on the left).[20] By contrast, the volatility of returns of relatively more liquid assets, such as sovereign bonds and equities, does not appear to be strongly affected by the liquidity of the funds that hold them.

The sensitivity of asset price fragility to fund vulnerabilities increases in periods of market stress. The analysis considers two measures of stress: (1) uncertainty (or fear) in financial markets, proxied by the Chicago Board Options Exchange Volatility (VIX) Index; and (2) US monetary

policy uncertainty.[21] The analysis shows that the previously documented adverse impact of asset-level vulnerability on bond return volatility is more pronounced when financial or monetary policy uncertainty is elevated (Figure 3.10, panel 1). A one standard deviation increase in the vulnerability measure is associated with about a 20 percent increase in bond return volatility (relative to median volatility) when the VIX Index or monetary policy uncertainty is high (at the 75th percentile of their distribution) relative to when they are low (at the 25th percentile of their distribution).

Notably, in periods of high macro-financial uncertainty, the return volatility of more liquid assets such as sovereign bonds also appears to increase. This could be consistent with funds following a "pecking order" when liquidating assets

[19]The analysis is robust to the use of security and issuer fixed effects combined with time fixed effects, which controls for time-varying issuer characteristics such as credit risk. See Online Annex 3.2 for a detailed description of the empirical approach and robustness tests.

[20]This finding is comparable to that reported by Jiang and others (2022), who find that a one standard deviation increase in the vulnerability of US corporate bonds is associated with a 16 percent higher return volatility.

[21]US monetary policy uncertainty is measured based on textual analysis of newspaper articles (Husted, Rogers, and Sun 2020). Based on this measure, monetary policy uncertainty was elevated in 2019 and has been rising since the end of 2021. The VIX Index spiked during the market turbulence in March 2020, when uncertainty about the effect of the COVID-19 pandemic was high (see Online Annex 3.2).

Figure 3.9. Open-End Investment Fund Vulnerabilities Contribute to Fragility in Corporate Bond Markets

Corporate bonds held by less liquid funds tend to experience significant return volatility, but more liquid asset classes, such as sovereign bonds or equities, do not.

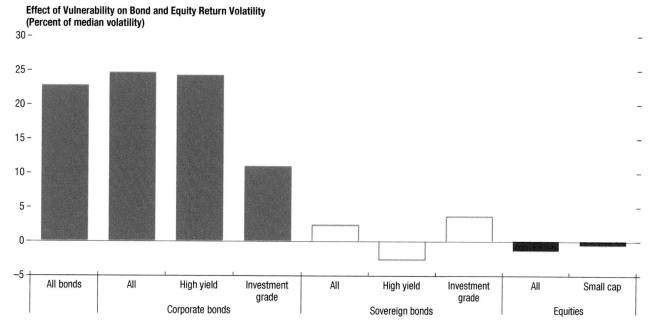

Effect of Vulnerability on Bond and Equity Return Volatility
(Percent of median volatility)

Sources: FactSet; Morningstar; Refinitiv; and IMF staff calculations.
Note: The figure shows the coefficient on the asset-level vulnerability measure in a regression of quarterly asset return volatility on the lagged vulnerability measure over the period 2013:Q4–2021:Q4. Asset-level vulnerability is calculated based on the illiquidity of the funds holding that asset (following Jiang and others 2022). Coefficients are shown by asset class. Asset return volatility is calculated based on weekly returns over one quarter and is expressed relative to the sample median of the respective asset class. Asset-level vulnerability is defined as a z-score (de-meaned and divided by the standard deviation of the respective subsample). For details of the estimated regression models, see Online Annex 3.2. Solid bars indicate statistical significance at 10 percent or lower.

in times of stress (Ma, Xiao, and Zeng 2022). Funds with sufficient liquid assets may sell those first to raise cash before selling their illiquid assets. In such cases, even otherwise liquid assets can become fragile.[22]

Herding can further amplify the effect of fund vulnerabilities on asset prices. As discussed earlier, the simultaneous selling of assets by investment funds that hold similar portfolios or have similar strategies and behaviors could drive asset prices away from fundamentals and induce more volatility, especially under strained market liquidity conditions. The results of the analysis show that this is indeed the case: the impact of fund-level illiquidity on volatility is higher for securities that experience higher levels of herding (where herding is measured as the

tendency of funds to trade in the same direction, following Cai and others 2019). A one standard deviation increase in the vulnerability measure has a 3 percent to 5 percent larger effect on return volatility (relative to the median) for securities exposed to sell-herding compared with those that are not exposed (Figure 3.10, panel 2).

Emerging markets are particularly vulnerable to sharp outflows from OEFs. Fund-level vulnerabilities in advanced economies tend to spill over to asset prices in emerging market economies, particularly to corporate bond prices (Figure 3.11, panel 1). A one standard deviation increase in the vulnerability measure of emerging market corporate bonds held by funds domiciled in advanced economies is associated with a 23 percent increase in their return volatility relative to their median volatility. The impact is magnified during market stress: a one standard deviation increase in vulnerability is associated with a 14 percent higher impact on bond return volatility

---

[22]Empirical analysis conducted later in the chapter supports the view that funds follow a pecking order of liquidation in times of stress.

Figure 3.10. Asset-Level Vulnerabilities Amplified by Market Stress and Herding

The return volatility of fixed-income assets held by more illiquid funds increases as macro-financial uncertainty rises.

Herding by funds can also amplify the adverse effect of vulnerabilities on return volatility.

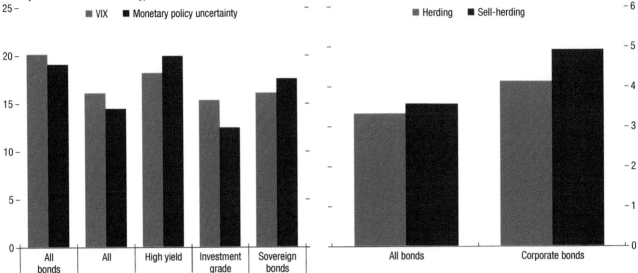

1. Differential Effect of Vulnerability on Bond Return Volatility in High- vs. Low-Stress Situations
(Percent of median volatility)

2. Differential Effect of Vulnerability on Bond Return Volatility for Securities with High vs. Low Herding
(Percent of median volatility)

Sources: FactSet; Morningstar; Refinitiv; and IMF staff calculations.
Note: Panel 1 shows the difference in the impact of the asset-level vulnerability measure on asset return volatility at high and low levels of the Chicago Board Options Exchange Volatility (VIX) Index and the monetary policy uncertainty measure (where high and low refer to the 75th and 25th percentiles of the sample distribution of the corresponding stress variables, respectively). Panel 2 shows the difference in the impact of the asset-level vulnerability measure on asset return volatility at high and low levels of sell-herding (where high and low are defined as the 75th and 25th percentiles of the sample distribution of the herding measure, respectively). The herding measure is based on Cai and others (2019); sell-herding considers only securities with more sellers than buyers. See Online Annex 3.2 for further details on the estimated regressions. Solid bars indicate statistical significance at 10 percent or lower.

in periods when the VIX Index is high compared with periods when it is low (Figure 3.11, panel 2).

These findings suggest that vulnerabilities associated with funds' liquidity mismatches generate fragility in asset markets, especially in fixed-income markets. The results also show that this fragility is amplified when macro-financial uncertainty is high and funds engage in herding. The next section will shed light on some of the underlying mechanisms through which fund vulnerabilities tend to influence asset return volatility.

Transmission of Risks from Open-End Investment Funds to Asset Price Fragility

An adverse shock can create a vicious circle, especially for less liquid funds, whereby investor redemptions force funds to liquidate portfolios, generating selling pressures that reduce the market

value of securities and lead to further redemptions. This vicious circle is illustrated in Figure 3.5, and the analysis confirms the empirical relevance of this mechanism through three main findings:

- Less liquid funds tend to face larger outflows, particularly during periods of high uncertainty and volatility, as measured by an increase in the VIX Index (Figure 3.12, panel 1).[23]
- Outflows from funds lead to selling pressure. Bonds with higher vulnerability—that is, those held by less liquid funds—are more likely to be liquidated when funds experience large outflows, with the effects being particularly pronounced for

---

[23]The higher sensitivity of fund outflows to fund illiquidity during periods of stress complements previous findings by Chen, Goldstein, and Jiang (2010) and Goldstein, Jiang, and Ng (2017), who show a stronger sensitivity of outflows to the poor performance of illiquid funds.

Figure 3.11. Spillovers from Advanced Economy Open-End Investment Funds to Asset Prices in Emerging Market Economies

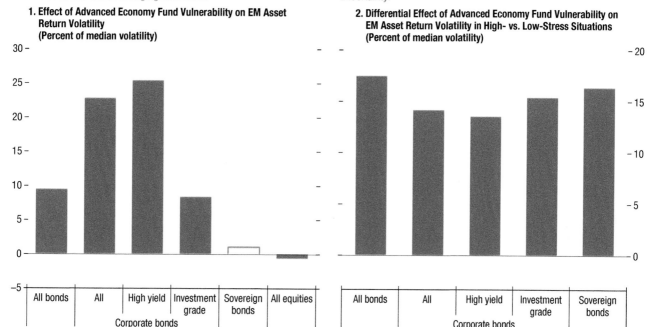

Vulnerabilities from funds domiciled in advanced economies can spill over to bond markets in emerging markets ...

1. Effect of Advanced Economy Fund Vulnerability on EM Asset Return Volatility
(Percent of median volatility)

... and the effect is particularly pronounced in periods of high financial uncertainty.

2. Differential Effect of Advanced Economy Fund Vulnerability on EM Asset Return Volatility in High- vs. Low-Stress Situations
(Percent of median volatility)

Sources: Morningstar; and IMF staff calculations.
Note: Panel 1 shows the spillover effect of vulnerabilities from funds domiciled in advanced economies on EM securities markets by regressing EM bond and equity return volatility on asset-level vulnerability measures that are calculated considering advanced economy funds only and relevant controls. Panel 2 shows the difference in the impact of the asset-level vulnerability measure at high and low levels of the Chicago Board Options Exchange Volatility Index (for which high and low refer to the 75th and 25th percentile of the sample distribution, respectively). See Online Annex 3.2 for a detailed description of the regression models. Solid bars indicate statistical significance at 10 percent or lower. EM = emerging market.

high-yield bonds (Figure 3.12, panel 2).[24] Further analysis shows that in periods of market stress, such as during the COVID-19 market turmoil, funds appear to follow a pecking order of liquidation, selling relatively more liquid assets within their portfolio first (Figure 3.12, panel 3).[25] This result

implies that selling pressure on funds can also have a sizable price impact on asset markets that are usually considered liquid (such as sovereign bonds) when uncertainty is high, as illustrated in Figure 3.10, panel 1.

• Selling pressures induced by fund outflows lead to significant price movements in the underlying assets. Estimating the impact of selling pressure on the abnormal returns of different assets during the COVID-19 market turmoil suggests that selling pressures can cause substantial price movements and negative abnormal returns for bonds (Figure 3.12, panel 4).[26]

[24]The selling pressure measure captures the difference between sales and purchases of bonds by OEFs that experience extreme outflows and inflows, respectively, with a large positive (negative) value indicating strong selling (buying) pressure.

[25]Such a pecking order—known as horizontal slicing—implies that the likelihood of a fund's sale of a given security depends not only on the absolute level of liquidity of the security but also on its liquidity relative to other assets in the fund's portfolio; that is, its liquidation rank (Ma, Xiao, and Zeng 2022). The liquidation rank of a security in a fund's portfolio corresponds to the portfolio share of other bonds held by the same fund that are less liquid. This implies, for example, that an investment-grade bond held by a high-yield fund might be among the first assets to be sold, while the same bond held by an investment-grade fund might be liquidated much later in the pecking order (as more liquid assets might be available in the investment-grade fund). See Online Annex 3.3 for further details.

[26]The measure of selling pressure used here accounts for funds' liquidation policies. Intuitively, the "liquidation-adjusted" outflow of two securities held by the same fund will depend on the pecking order followed by the fund, since securities higher up in the pecking order are more likely to be sold by the fund to raise the cash needed when facing outflows.

Figure 3.12. Transmission Channels of Open-End Investment Fund Vulnerabilities

Illiquid funds tend to face larger outflows, especially at high levels of stress.

1. Effect of Fund Illiquidity on Fund Outflows by Level of Financial Stress
(Percent of fund size)

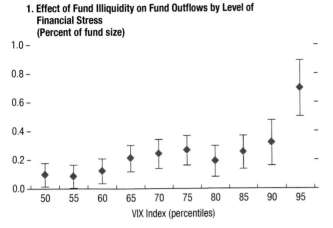

Assets held by less liquid funds face stronger selling pressures.

2. Effect of Fund Vulnerabilities on Selling Pressures
(Percent of average sell-off pressure)

During periods of market stress, more liquid securities are more likely to be sold first following large investor redemptions ...

3. Pecking Order and Sensitivity of Liquidations to Fund Outflows during the COVID-19 Market Turmoil
(Percentage points)

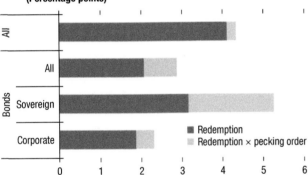

... and subsequent selling pressure can lead to significant price movements in the underlying assets.

4. Effect of Fund Outflows on Asset Returns during the COVID-19 Market Turmoil
(Percentage points)

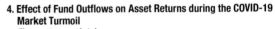
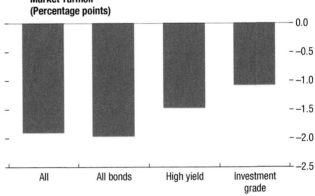

Sources: Bloomberg Finance L.P.; FactSet; Haver Analytics; Morningstar; and IMF staff calculations.
Note: Panel 1 shows the results of fund-level panel regressions in which outflows from funds are regressed on fund-level illiquidity measures while controlling for fund-level characteristics and country-time fixed effects. The results are presented at different levels of market stress identified as periods when the Chicago Board Options Exchange Volatility (VIX) Index is above a given percentile of its sample distribution. Error bars correspond to 90 percent confidence intervals. In panels 2–4, "All" refers to all securities in the sample, including equities. Panel 2 shows the effect of the asset-level vulnerability measure on selling pressures of assets over the sample period. The indicator of selling pressure is constructed following Jiang and others (2022) and is based on realized fund trades conditional on large fund flows to capture selling pressures for a given asset. A large positive (negative) value of the measure indicates strong selling (buying) pressure. The value of the estimated coefficient for high-yield corporate bonds is equal to 46 percent (the y-axis is truncated for visual clarity). Panels 3 and 4 show the results of an event study analysis focusing on the COVID-19–induced market turmoil in the first quarter of 2020. Panel 3 shows the effect of 10 percent fund outflows ("redemptions") on securities liquidations when the outflow is interacted with a fund-security-level pecking order indicator for each security. The pecking order of a security in a given fund's portfolio corresponds to its liquidation rank as defined in Ma, Xiao, and Zeng (2022). It is computed for each asset held by a given fund as the total portfolio share of other securities held by the same fund that are relatively less liquid (that is, have a higher bid-ask spread). Panel 4 shows the effect of liquidation-adjusted outflows from funds on abnormal returns of different assets. Abnormal returns are calculated as the difference between a security's return and the average return of assets with a similar maturity and rating. Solid bars indicate statistical significance at 10 percent or lower. See Online Annex 3.2 for a detailed description of the variables and empirical methodology.

Figure 3.13. Open-End Investment Fund Vulnerabilities and Financial Conditions

An increase in asset holdings by more illiquid open-end investment funds is associated with tighter financial conditions ...

... and the relationship is stronger when financial conditions are tight.

Fund vulnerabilities imply negative cross-border spillovers for EMs.

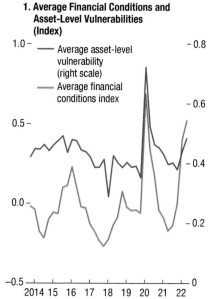

1. Average Financial Conditions and Asset-Level Vulnerabilities (Index)

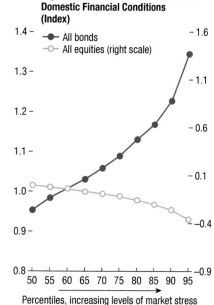

2. Impact of Asset-Level Vulnerabilities on Domestic Financial Conditions (Index)

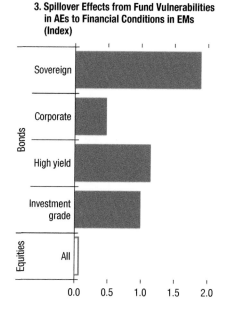

3. Spillover Effects from Fund Vulnerabilities in AEs to Financial Conditions in EMs (Index)

Sources: Bloomberg Finance L.P.; FactSet; Haver Analytics; Morningstar; and IMF staff calculations.
Note: Panel 1 shows the average asset-level vulnerability and domestic financial conditions index across countries. Higher values of the financial conditions index indicate a tightening of financial conditions. The index is set to zero at its historical average. See Online Appendix 3.2 for a description of the domestic financial conditions index. Panels 2–3 show the results from country-level panel regressions with fixed effects in which the domestic financial conditions index in period $t + 1$ is regressed on asset-level vulnerabilities averaged at the issuer-country level in period t. Panel 2 is estimated using panel quantile regressions to assess the relationship between financial conditions and fund vulnerabilities at different levels of market stress. The model controls for domestic macro-financial factors and external shocks such as domestic and US monetary policy shocks, average GDP growth of foreign economies, changes in global liquidity conditions, and commodity price shocks. In panel 3, spillover analysis is performed by substituting domestic fund vulnerabilities with a measure capturing foreign fund vulnerabilities, which is computed as the average asset-level vulnerability from holdings of funds domiciled in advanced economies. Panel 3 shows the effect when restricting the country-level panel regressions to EMs. Solid dots and solid bars indicate statistical significance at 10 percent or lower. AE = advanced economy; EM = emerging market.

Spillovers to Financial Markets from Vulnerabilities in Open-End Investment Funds

Through their effect on asset prices, fund vulnerabilities may generate broader macro-financial stability risks. As shown in the previous section, investor redemptions from funds lead to selling pressure that increases market volatility and depresses asset prices. The reduction in asset prices could in turn adversely affect the balance sheets of other financial and nonfinancial entities and lead to a broader tightening of financial conditions, generating macro-financial stability risks. A preliminary look at the data suggests that average financial conditions across countries are indeed correlated with average asset-level vulnerability (the extent to which assets are held by illiquid funds).

That is, financial conditions appear to tighten with an increase in asset holdings by less liquid OEFs, and vice versa (Figure 3.13, panel 1).

Formal empirical analysis confirms that fund vulnerabilities can lead to market-wide effects, and that the strength of the relationship varies with the level of market stress.[27] On average, an increase in the vulnerability measure for less liquid assets such as bonds is associated with a significant tightening of financial

---

[27]Country-level panel regressions are estimated looking at the impact of average asset-level vulnerabilities (that is, the extent to which domestic securities are held by more illiquid funds) on future domestic financial conditions while controlling for other relevant domestic and external factors such as domestic and US monetary policy shocks, average GDP growth of foreign economies, changes in global liquidity conditions, and commodity price shocks.

Figure 3.14. Availability and Implementation of Liquidity Management Tools

The availability and implementation of liquidity management tools vary across jurisdictions.

Share of Funds with Available Liquidity Management Tools, 2021:Q4
(Percent of total fund size)

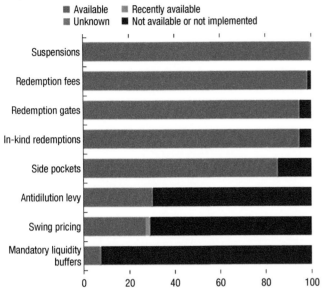

Sources: European Securities and Markets Authority (2020); International Organization of Securities Commissions (2015); Morningstar; and IMF staff calculations.
Note: Bars represent the total net assets of funds across jurisdictions that can and do implement liquidity management tools.

conditions in the next period (Figure 3.13, panel 2). No similar effect is visible for more liquid equity securities. Furthermore, this effect is amplified as financial conditions tighten.

The impact of fund vulnerabilities in source countries can also spill over to financial conditions in recipient economies. On average, increased holdings of domestic assets by nonresident advanced economy illiquid funds are associated with significant tightening in domestic financial conditions of recipient countries in the period that follows (Figure 3.13, panel 3). While such spillover effects from advanced economy funds are present for the full sample of countries, they are much stronger for emerging market economies (Online Annex Figure 3.2.2).

Overall, these results show that OEFs can transmit shocks to financial conditions, both domestically and

across borders. Reducing the vulnerabilities associated with these funds could thus help mitigate asset price fragility and risks to macro-financial stability. In this context, the next section looks at the role that liquidity risk management tools can play to enhance the resilience of the sector.

Liquidity Management Tools to Address the Risks from Open-End Investment Funds

Liquidity management tools can potentially reduce the vulnerabilities associated with OEFs and mitigate their potential to amplify asset price fragility. The availability of liquidity management tools varies by jurisdiction, but in general a wide range of tools is available to OEFs across all major jurisdictions (Figure 3.14). Tools that limit investors' ability to redeem when funds experience severe outflows—such as redemption suspensions, redemption fees, redemption gates, or in-kind redemptions—are the most widely available. However, these are generally deployed only in periods of extreme market stress, and funds tend to be concerned about the stigma associated with their use.[28] Antidilution levies and swing pricing are tools that can potentially reduce OEF vulnerabilities ex ante by passing on transaction costs (including asset liquidation costs) to investors exiting the fund, thus reducing their incentives to run. However, antidilution levies and swing pricing are available only in a limited number of jurisdictions, and their utilization remains limited.[29] Mandatory requirements on holding minimum liquidity buffers appear to be the least-used tools across jurisdictions.

---

[28]For example, Grill, Vivar, and Wedow (2021) document that during the COVID-19 market turmoil, at least 215 funds suspended redemptions and that those funds subsequently experienced larger outflows than comparable funds, suggesting reputational costs associated with fund suspensions.

[29]Swing pricing is commonly used by funds in Europe (Bank of England and Financial Conduct Authority 2021; European Securities and Markets Authority 2020) but has not been implemented by funds in the United States, despite approval to do so by the Securities and Exchange Commission in 2018. A key reason for this lack of adoption in the United States is that funds there may not necessarily know the size of net flows into the fund before the price of a fund is determined. This precludes them from applying a swing factor that is based on net flows.

Figure 3.15. Liquid Asset Holdings of Open-End Investment Funds

Cash buffers vary widely within and across funds ...

... but tend to increase with the illiquidity of a fund's portfolio, with no notable difference between funds that use swing pricing and those that do not.

Funds appear to rely less on cash buffers to manage investor redemptions in periods of stress.

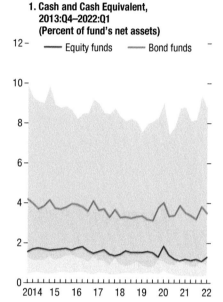

1. Cash and Cash Equivalent, 2013:Q4–2022:Q1
(Percent of fund's net assets)

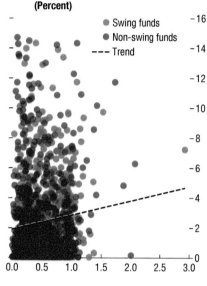

2. Cash and Cash Equivalent Holdings and Portfolio Illiquidity
(Percent)

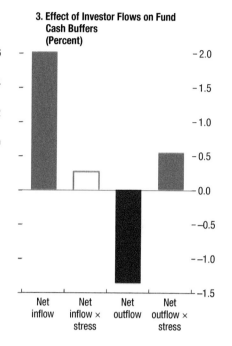

3. Effect of Investor Flows on Fund Cash Buffers
(Percent)

Sources: Morningstar; and IMF staff calculations.
Note: Cash and cash equivalents include cash held in bank accounts as well as certificates of deposit, currency, money market holdings, and other high-quality fixed-income securities with a maturity of less than 92 days. Panel 1 shows the median level of cash and cash equivalents relative to a fund's total net assets, and the green and yellow areas indicate the interquartile range. Panel 2 shows the average portfolio illiquidity of funds (over the sample) relative to their cash holdings in percent of total net assets. Panel 3 shows the coefficients from a regression of the percentage change in fund-level cash holdings on net inflows as a percent of fund assets, net outflows as a percent of fund assets, and interaction terms with a stress dummy equal to 1 when the Chicago Board Options Exchange Volatility Index is above its 90th sample percentile. Net inflows are equal to positive net fund flows and zero otherwise. Net outflows are calculated as the negative of net fund flows when fund flows are negative and are zero otherwise. See Online Annex 3.4 for further details on the regression models and variables. Solid bars indicate statistical significance at 10 percent or lower.

There is no clear consensus yet on the effectiveness of liquidity buffers in mitigating fund vulnerabilities.[30] Liquidity buffers could provide funds with additional flexibility to time their asset sales when facing outflows. However, they do not eliminate the first-mover advantage and can also adversely impact long-term fund performance by constraining the capacity of

funds to provide investors with exposure to particular investment themes or asset classes.

In general, funds holding relatively less liquid securities tend to have higher cash buffers, even if not mandated. Liquidity buffers of OEFs vary widely across and within fund types, ranging from 0.5 percent to 4 percent for equity funds and from 1 percent to 9 percent for bond funds (Figure 3.15, panel 1). Funds holding relatively illiquid securities—as measured by their bid-ask spread—on average hold larger cash buffers, which could provide them with the ability to pay redeeming investors without forcing asset sales in stressed market conditions (Figure 3.15, panel 2). There is, however, no meaningful difference between the cash holdings of funds that use swing pricing as a liquidity management tool and those

---

[30]For example, Giuzio and others (2021) argue that cash buffers can reduce run risks and costly sales of illiquid assets. Di Lasio, Kaufmann and Wicknig (2022) argue that liquidity buffers could reduce bond sales by funds that are hit by large redemptions. However, dynamic cash rebuilding by funds after outflows could also exacerbate rather than reduce run risks (Zeng 2017). Jiang, Li, and Wang (2021) further show that corporate bond funds may not necessarily use their more liquid asset holdings relative to illiquid assets during periods of market stress to maintain portfolio liquidity.

Figure 3.16. Effectiveness of Swing Pricing in Reducing Asset Price Fragility

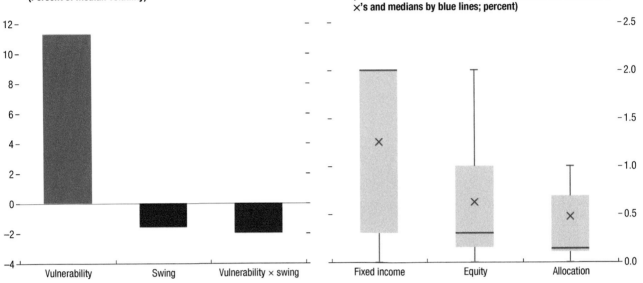

Swing pricing can partially mitigate asset price fragility due to fund vulnerabilities.

However, swing factors are often capped at low levels, potentially reducing their effectiveness in periods of market stress.

1. Effect of Swing Pricing on Bond Return Volatility
(Percent of median volatility)

2. Maximum Downward Swing Factor among 200 Sample Funds
(Boxes cover the 25th–75th percentiles; means are denoted by ×'s and medians by blue lines; percent)

Sources: FactSet; Morningstar; Refinitiv; and IMF staff calculations.
Note: Panel 1 shows the coefficients from a regression of return volatility on asset-level vulnerabilities and an asset-level swing pricing exposure variable, in which swing pricing funds are defined as funds domiciled in Luxembourg or the United Kingdom. Effects are based on weekly asset price volatilities. See Online Annex 3.2 for further details on the empirical framework. Solid bars indicate statistical significance at 10 percent or lower.

that do not. Analyzing the impact of redemptions on funds' cash buffers suggests that in normal times funds facing outflows deplete their cash buffers to pay out investors, though this does not necessarily hold in times of severe market stress, when funds appear to preserve the liquidity of their portfolios (Figure 3.15, panel 3).[31]

Swing pricing appears to be an effective tool to reduce fund-induced asset price fragility, but calibration is key. In contrast to ex post liquidity management tools such as gates or suspensions, which address runs on funds once they occur, swing pricing is an ex ante tool that eliminates first-mover advantages in OEFs by directly imposing the transaction costs associated with redemptions on the redeeming investors (such as in ETFs; Box 3.1). However, this requires "swing factors" (that is, the adjustment factor applied to the fund price at which investors can redeem or subscribe to mutual fund shares) to be calibrated to

reflect the full cost of outflows, including the price impact of asset liquidations.[32] This calibration could be challenging for highly illiquid assets or in periods of extreme market stress when assessing the price impact of trades may be difficult due to price dislocation.[33]

Swing pricing mitigates vulnerabilities from OEFs, but investor run risks remain if swing factors are set too low. The chapter's analysis shows that the adverse impact of fund vulnerabilities on the volatility of bond returns is reduced by about one-third if more funds implement swing pricing (Figure 3.16, panel 1).[34] However, this mitigating effect is not

[31]This finding is consistent with Jiang, Li, and Wang (2021), who show that during tranquil market conditions, corporate bond funds tend to reduce liquid asset holdings to meet investor redemptions, but in periods with heightened uncertainty, they tend to preserve portfolio liquidity.

[32]Antidilution levies can have a similar effect by imposing a fee on redeeming investors.

[33]The expected price impact will depend not only on the trading needs of a single fund but also on those of other funds, making it particularly difficult for funds to accurately estimate price impact in times of stress. Optimally, swing factors would incorporate the trading behaviors of the overall fund sector.

[34]This result is in line with Jin and others (2022), who show that swing pricing can eliminate the first-mover advantage arising from the traditional pricing rule and significantly reduce outflows during market stress. However, the result of swing pricing needs to be interpreted with caution because limited data about the use of swing pricing by funds make it difficult to accurately identify its effect. The empirical analysis proxies for swing pricing by classifying funds domiciled in countries where swing pricing is ubiquitous as

sufficient to fully offset the increase in return volatility induced by illiquid funds' holdings of the bonds.[35] The limited effectiveness of swing pricing could be the result of insufficient calibration of the swing factor. Studies estimating the optimal swing factor for OEFs that would fully eliminate run risks and the associated vulnerabilities find it to be in the range of 0 to 9 percent, with the higher end of the range applying to periods of stress when price impact is high and for funds whose investors react strongly to poor performance (Capponi, Glasserman, and Weber 2020; Anadu and others 2022).[36] Currently, many funds are constrained by maximum swing factors, which they typically set substantially below 9 percent (Figure 3.16, panel 2) and define in their prospectuses.[37] These caps tend to be set based on direct trading costs, such as commissions and bid-ask spreads, without fully accounting for indirect costs such as the price impact of asset sales. Funds may also set the swing factors low out of competitive pressure because some investors may value liquidity provision and prefer funds with low caps on the size of the swing factors. Such caps may limit the ability of funds to adjust swing factors sufficiently to cover the impact of redemptions in times of stress on asset prices, thereby reducing the effectiveness of swing pricing in eliminating run risk.

Conclusion and Policy Recommendations

Open-end investment funds play an increasingly important role in financial markets but raise financial stability concerns. The share of global financial assets held by OEFs has grown dramatically over the past two decades. However, vulnerabilities associated with the liquidity mismatch between their asset holdings and liabilities can subject some funds to investor run risk that can lead to severe dislocations in financial markets and amplify the adverse macro-financial impact of exogenous shocks.

The analysis in this chapter shows that OEFs holding illiquid assets that offer daily redemptions to investors are a key driver of asset price fragility. The most affected assets are those in less liquid markets, such as corporate bonds. The volatility of their returns increases significantly—especially in times of market stress—if these assets are held by more illiquid funds. The impact of fund vulnerabilities can have significant cross-border spillover effects and lead to greater asset price volatility in emerging market economies. They may also have system-wide implications by contributing to a tightening of domestic financial conditions, thereby reinforcing the vicious cycle between redemptions, fund asset sales, and the price impact of these sales.

Policy action is needed to mitigate the risks associated with OEFs. A wide range of liquidity management tools is available that could potentially mitigate the vulnerabilities associated with OEFs and reduce their systemic impact, but effective implementation of these tools is lacking.

Policy tools that limit vulnerabilities ex ante by reducing the risk of investor runs may be preferable to those that attempt to mitigate the impact of such runs once they are underway. Liquidity management tools that limit investors' ability to redeem—such as redemption suspensions or gates—do not address the intrinsic first-mover advantage problem associated with some OEFs and are typically adopted by funds already facing significant outflow pressures, which may limit their effectiveness in mitigating systemic risks.[38] Holding cash and other liquidity buffers may give funds the flexibility to respond to shocks but do not necessarily reduce the risk of investor runs and hence may also be insufficient to address the systemic risks associated with less liquid OEFs.[39] By contrast, price-based tools, such as swing pricing or antidilution

---

"swinging funds" and the rest as "nonswinging funds." See Online Annex 3.2 for a description of the empirical methodology.

[35]These results capture only the direct effect from funds' adoption of swing pricing on the price volatility of bonds in their portfolio. The introduction of swing pricing at the fund level likely offers additional benefits by reducing run risks for other funds holding similar assets, thereby stabilizing the fund market segment as a whole.

[36]Capponi, Glasserman, and Weber (2020) calibrate the optimal swing factor as a function of the direct price impact on assets that would result from funds' transactions following investor redemptions. Anadu and others (2022) consider ETF premiums and discounts to derive the optimal swing factors for funds investing in short-term corporate bonds. The latter approach may have several limitations because ETF premiums and discounts may also be driven by factors such as the ability of authorized participants to provide liquidity. In addition, ETF investors may differ (have different liquidity preferences) from OEF investors.

[37]In most jurisdictions where swing pricing is permitted, funds are required to publish the maximum swing factors they may apply in their prospectus and cannot apply a larger swing factor without changing the prospectus.

[38]Such tools could even exacerbate run risks because investors may try to redeem before the measures are applied by the fund.

[39]Tools such as redemption suspensions and liquidity buffers may also be less desirable from an end-investor perspective because they restrict access to liquidity and constrain funds' investment mandates, respectively.

levies, can reduce investors' incentives to front-run others by passing on transaction costs to redeeming investors, thereby protecting investors and mitigating systemic risks. However, more widespread adoption by funds and appropriate calibration of these tools is key to their effectiveness.

Policy interventions may be necessary to ensure that price-based measures are set at adequate levels, especially in periods of stress and poor market liquidity. Swing pricing, for example, has been a market-led innovation in many jurisdictions, introduced to protect investors from the dilution of their fund shares. However, fund-imposed caps on swing factors could constrain funds' ability to fully pass on the transaction costs to redeeming investors and, thus far, may have limited the effectiveness of swing pricing as a macroprudential tool in times of stress. Funds could therefore be required to eliminate caps and to calibrate swing factors such that they fully reflect the price impact of a fund's asset sales.[40] Policymakers should further investigate how to enhance the effectiveness of swing pricing and other price-based liquidity management tools—for example, by encouraging the disclosure of swing pricing practices and calibration methodologies and by improving the availability of aggregate fund flow data in real time to help funds determine the appropriate swing factors, especially during times of stress. Tighter monitoring of liquidity risk management practices by supervisors and regulators should also be considered to ensure the appropriate implementation of liquidity management tools. To this end, the collection of additional data on funds' liquidity risks may be necessary.

Other liquidity management tools could include linking the frequency of redemptions to the liquidity of funds' portfolios in order to directly address the underlying vulnerability related to liquidity mismatch. This option may be suitable for funds holding very illiquid assets (for example, real estate) for which the appropriate calibration of price-based tools is difficult even in normal times. It may also be suitable for funds

based in jurisdictions where price-based tools cannot be effectively implemented for operational reasons. In such cases, investors could be offered the opportunity to redeem early in exchange for a redemption fee that is calibrated to reflect stress conditions and prevent dilution of the shares of remaining investors.

Given the adverse cross-border spillover effects of fund vulnerabilities, recipient countries will also need to take appropriate policy steps to mitigate potential systemic risks arising from the volatility of capital flows sourced from international funds. Recipient countries need to be mindful of the volatility of capital flows originating from funds in advanced economies and emphasize continued deepening of domestic markets; appropriate use of debt management tools; and use of macroeconomic, prudential, capital flow management, and foreign exchange intervention tools in line with the IMF's Institutional View to address risks arising from surges and sharp reversals in portfolio investments by OEFs (IMF 2012, 2022).

Policymakers should further analyze exchange-traded funds (ETFs) which do not appear to be subject to the same liquidity vulnerabilities as OEFs (Box 3.1). Empirical analysis shows that bonds held by ETFs experience a smaller increase in volatility during periods of stress than comparable bonds held by OEFs. However, other evidence also shows that ETFs can increase nonfundamental volatility in asset markets and amplify the sensitivity of cross-border capital flows to global financial conditions.

Policymakers should put in place adequate disclosure requirements to allow for a proper assessment of the role of leverage in amplifying vulnerabilities from OEFs (IMF 2021). At present, the reporting of leverage, especially via the use of derivatives (synthetic leverage), is limited, which prevents a comprehensive assessment of its role in contributing to OEF vulnerabilities.

Policymakers should consider measures to bolster the provision of liquidity and market resilience. Regardless of the vulnerabilities associated with some OEFs, large-scale redemptions and asset sales by OEFs or other market participants could result in fire sales and dislocation of asset prices if markets are not sufficiently liquid. Measures to improve liquidity provision, such as encouraging central clearing and supporting greater transparency in bond trading, should be considered to reduce risks from liquidity mismatch in OEFs and to support the functioning of securities

---

[40]In periods of extreme stress when market liquidity is very poor, swing factors or antidilution levies may be very large or difficult to calibrate. In such cases, redemption suspensions or gates may be an alternative, easier-to-implement tool. In a similar vein, IMF (2021) proposes a "waterfall" approach of progressively more aggressive liquidity management tools, such as redemption deferrals in case of moderate shocks, followed by in-kind redemption for moderate to large shocks, and market-wide fees or gates for large shocks.

markets in periods of stress (see the April 2015 GFSR and IMF 2021).

Competitive pressure and concerns about stigma may prevent funds from voluntarily implementing optimal policy solutions; policymakers should therefore consider mandating the adoption of liquidity management tools and enhanced disclosure. Over the past 15 years, central banks have had to intervene several times in financial markets during stress episodes to provide emergency liquidity support. To the extent that entities not included in the traditional regulatory perimeter continue to benefit from such support, policymakers may have to consider more extensive regulation of investment funds in the absence of adequate liquidity management practices to limit financial stability risks. Given the global operations of funds and their cross-border spillover effects, liquidity management practices should be deployed consistently at the global level to ensure their effectiveness, which calls for greater international regulatory coordination.

Box 3.1. Exchange-Traded Funds Generate Less Asset Price Fragility but May Also Be Vulnerable

Exchange-traded funds (ETFs) allow investors to buy and sell shares within a trading day, but unlike open-end investment funds (OEFs) they are not vulnerable to investor runs. ETFs have grown rapidly and constitute a substantial part of the investment fund universe (Figure 3.1.1, panel 1). They differ from OEFs in that they do not guarantee investors the ability to redeem shares at the funds' net asset value (that is, the price at the end of the trading day). Instead, ETFs are traded continuously in secondary markets at varying prices. These market prices are determined primarily by supply and demand for the ETF, and investors bear their own transaction costs when buying or selling. As a result, ETFs are not subject to the same first-mover advantage that gives rise to run risk

The author of this box is Anna-Theresa Helmke.

in OEFs. Empirical analysis shows that bonds held by ETFs experience less of an increase in volatility during periods of stress than comparable bonds held by OEFs (Figure 3.1.1, panel 2).

ETF discounts reflect market liquidity costs. ETF prices are tied to the ETFs' net asset value through an arbitrage mechanism. Authorized participants, which tend to be large broker dealers, have the exclusive right to create and redeem ETF shares in exchange for a basket of portfolio securities. This process ensures that the secondary market price of ETFs remains close to the fund's net asset value. However, when market liquidity deteriorates and the balance sheets of broker dealers are constrained such that they may be limited in their ability to match buyers and sellers (that is, make markets), the gap between the net asset value and the ETF's share price could increase (Pan and

Figure 3.1.1. Asset Price Fragility and Exchange-Traded Funds

Inflows of ETFs have been large over the past decade.

In periods of stress, ownership by OEFs is associated with higher asset price fragility than ownership of ETFs ...

... and at the same time, ETF discounts tend to increase when aggregate liquidity deteriorates.

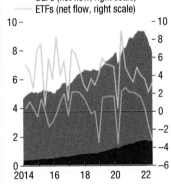

1. Total Net Assets and Flows of Bond ETFs and OEFs
(Trillions of US dollars; percent of total lagged net assets)

- OEFs (total net assets, left scale)
- ETFs (total net assets, left scale)
- OEFs (net flow, right scale)
- ETFs (net flow, right scale)

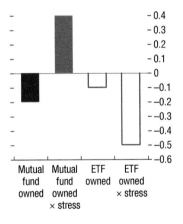

2. Effect of OEF Ownership and ETF Ownership on Bond Return Volatility
(Percent of median volatility)

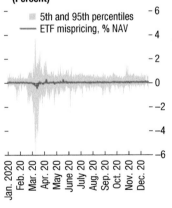

3. Difference between ETF Price and Fund Net Asset Value in Percent of the Fund Net Asset Value for Bond ETFs
(Percent)

- 5th and 95th percentiles
- ETF mispricing, % NAV

Sources: FactSet; Morningstar; Refinitiv; and IMF staff calculations.
Note: Panel 2 shows the coefficients from a regression of return volatility on asset ownership and an interaction term between asset ownership and a stress dummy equal to 1 when the Chicago Board Options Exchange Volatility (VIX) Index is above its 90th sample percentile and zero otherwise. "Mutual fund owned" refers to the total amount of an asset held by OEFs, but not by ETFs, as a percentage of its market capitalization. Effects are based on weekly asset price volatilities. The regression includes asset and issuer fixed effects. Standard errors are clustered at the asset and quarter levels. Solid bars indicate statistical significance at 10 percent or lower. Panel 3 shows the distribution of ETF mispricing for the sample of bond ETFs domiciled in the United States or Luxembourg. ETF mispricing is calculated at daily frequency as the difference between the ETF closing price and the fund NAV divided by the fund NAV. ETF = exchange-traded fund; OEF = open-end investment fund; NAV = net asset value.

Box 3.1 *(continued)*

Zeng 2019). Similar to the way in which mutual funds pass on transaction costs to redeeming investors when using swing pricing, this difference between the net asset value and the ETF price (referred to as the *ETF discount*) reflects transaction costs borne by investors who want to buy or sell the ETF. For example, during the March 2020 stress episode, when liquidity conditions were poor, the discounts on ETFs increased dramatically, reaching more than 5 percent across all bond ETFs (up to 27 percent for high-yield bond ETFs and up to 13 percent for investment-grade bond ETFs; see Figure 3.1.1, panel 3). These discounts are indicative of the swing factor that would be required by an OEF with a similar portfolio structure and investor base.

ETFs are also subject to vulnerabilities. The provision of intraday liquidity by ETFs makes them attractive for liquidity traders with short-term horizons. Together with the arbitrage activities of authorized participants who create and redeem ETF shares, this facilitates the transmission of nonfundamental shocks from short-term liquidity traders to securities markets. Consistent with this transmission, ETFs can increase nonfundamental volatility in asset markets (Ben-David, Franzoni, and Moussawi 2018) and amplify the sensitivity of cross-border capital flows to global financial conditions (Converse, Levy-Yeyati, and Williams 2020). Moreover, leveraged and inverse ETFs that rely on derivatives and short sales to amplify returns can introduce additional volatility in securities markets because of the need to rebalance the leveraged positions at the end of the trading day.

References

Anadu, Kenechukwu, John Levin, Victoria Liu, Noam Tanner, Antoine Malfroy-Camine, and Sean Baker. 2022. "Swing Pricing Calibration: A Simple Thought Exercise Using ETF Pricing Dynamics to Infer Swing Factors for Mutual Funds." Federal Reserve Bank of Boston.

Arslanalp, Serkan, Dimitris Drakopoulos, Rohit Goel, and Robin Koepke. 2020. "Benchmark-Driven Investments in Emerging Market Bond Markets: Taking Stock." IMF Working Paper 2020/192, International Monetary Fund, Washington, DC.

Bank of England (BoE) and Financial Conduct Authority (FCA). 2021. "Liquidity Management in UK Open-Ended Funds." London.

Ben-David, Itzhak, Francesco Franzoni, and Rabih Moussawi. 2018. "Do ETFs Increase Volatility?" *Journal of Finance* 73 (6): 2471–535.

Brown, Nerissa C., Kelsey D. Wei, and Russ Wermers. 2014. "Analyst Recommendations, Mutual Fund Herding, and Overreaction in Stock Prices." *Management Science* 60 (1): 1–20.

Cai, Fang, Song Han, Dan Li, and Yi Li. 2019. "Institutional Herding and Its Price Impact: Evidence from the Corporate Bond Market." *Journal of Financial Economics* 131 (1): 139–67.

Capponi, Agostino, Paul Glasserman, and Marko Weber. 2020. "Swing Pricing for Mutual Funds: Breaking the Feedback Loop between Fire Sales and Fund Redemptions." *Management Science* 66 (8): 3581–602.

Chen, Qi, Itay Goldstein, and Wei Jiang. 2010. "Payoff Complementarities and Financial Fragility: Evidence from Mutual Fund Outflows." *Journal of Financial Economics* 97 (2): 239–62.

Choi, Jaewon, Saeid Hoseinzade, Sean Seunghun Shin, and Hassan Tehranian. 2020. "Corporate Bond Mutual Funds and Asset Fire Sales." *Journal of Financial Economics* 138 (2): 432–57.

Converse, Nathan, Eduardo Levy-Yeyati, and Tomas Williams. 2020. "How ETFs Amplify the Global Financial Cycle in Emerging Markets." Board of Governors of the Federal Reserve System International Finance Discussion Paper 1268, Washington, DC.

Coval, Joshua, and Erik Stafford. 2007. "Asset Fire Sales (and Purchases) in Equity Markets." *Journal of Financial Economics* 86 (2): 479–512.

Di Lasio, Giovanni, Christoph Kaufmann, and Florian Wicknig. 2022. "Macroprudential Regulation of Investment Funds". ECB Working Paper Series No 2695/August 2022.

Emter, Lorenz, Falko Fecht, and Oana Peia. 2022. "Financial Fragility in Open-Ended Mutual Funds: The Role of Liquidity Management Tools." Paper presented at the Financial Stability Board—Conference on Understanding and Addressing Systemic Risks in NBFIs, Basel and online, June 8–9.

European Securities and Markets Authority (ESMA). 2020. "Recommendation of the European Systemic Risk Board (ESRB) on Liquidity Risk in Investment Funds." Paris.

Falato, Antonio, Itay Goldstein, and Ali Hortaçsu. 2021. "Financial Fragility in the COVID-19 Crisis: The Case of Investment Funds in Corporate Bond Markets." *Journal of Monetary Economics* 123: 35–52.

Financial Stability Board (FSB). 2021. "Global Monitoring Report on Non-Bank Financial Intermediation." Basel.

Financial Stability Board (FSB). 2022. "US Dollar Funding and Emerging Market Economy Vulnerabilities." Basel. www.fsb.org/wp-content/uploads/P260422.pdf

Giuzio, Margherita, Michael Grill, Dominika Kryczka, and Christian Weistroffer. 2021. "A Theoretical Model Analysing Investment Funds' Liquidity Management and Policy Measures." Macroprudential Bulletin 12, European Central Bank, Frankfurt.

Goldstein, Itay, Hao Jiang, and David T. Ng. 2017. "Investor Flows and Fragility in Corporate Bond Funds." *Journal of Financial Economics* 126 (3): 592–613.

Greenwood, Robin, and David Thesmar. 2011. "Stock Price Fragility." *Journal of Financial Economics* 102 (3): 471–90.

Grill, Michael, Luis Molestina Vivar, and Michael Wedow. 2021. "The Suspensions of Redemptions during the COVID-19 Crisis—A Case for Pre-Emptive Liquidity Measures?" Macroprudential Bulletin 12, European Central Bank, Frankfurt.

Hespeler, Frank, and Felix Suntheim. 2020. "The Behavior of Fixed-Income Funds during COVID-19 Market Turmoil." Global Financial Stability Note 2020/002, International Monetary Fund, Washington, DC.

Husted, Lucas, John Rogers, and Bo Sun. 2020. "Monetary Policy Uncertainty." *Journal of Monetary Economics* 115: 20–36.

International Monetary Fund (IMF). 2012. "The Liberalization and Management of Capital Flows: An Institutional View." Policy Paper, Washington, DC.

International Monetary Fund (IMF). 2021. "Investment Funds and Financial Stability: Policy Considerations." Departmental Paper 2021/018, Washington, DC.

International Monetary Fund (IMF). 2022. "Review of the Institutional View on the Liberalization and Management of Capital Flows." IMF Policy Paper No. 2022/008, Washington, DC.

International Organization of Securities Commissions (IOSCO). 2015. "Liquidity Management Tools in Collective Investment Schemes. Results from an IOSCO Committee 5 Survey to Members." IOSCO Paper FR28/2015, Madrid. www.iosco.org/library/pubdocs/pdf/IOSCOPD517.pdf

Jiang, Hao, Dan Li, and Ashley Wang. 2021. "Dynamic Liquidity Management by Corporate Bond Mutual Funds." *Journal of Financial and Quantitative Analysis* 56 (5): 1622–52.

Jiang, Hao, Yi Li, Zheng Sun, and Ashley Wang. 2022. "Does Mutual Fund Illiquidity Introduce Fragility into Asset Prices? Evidence from the Corporate Bond Market." *Journal of Financial Economics* 143 (1): 277–302.

Jin, Dunhong, Marcin Kacperczyk, Bige Kahraman, and
   Felix Suntheim. 2022. "Swing Pricing and Fragil-
   ity in Open-End Mutual Funds." *Review of Financial
   Studies* 35 (1): 1–50.

Lewrick, Ulf, Jochen Schanz, Jean-François Carpantier, and
   Shaneera Rasqué. 2022. "An Assessment of Investment Funds'
   Liquidity Management Tools." CSSF Working Paper, Com-
   mission de Surveillance du Secteur Financier, Luxembourg.

Liang, Nellie. 2020. "Corporate Bond Market Dysfunction during COVID-19 and Lessons from the Fed's
   Responses." Hutchins Center Working Paper 69, Brookings Institution, Washington, DC. www.brookings.edu/wp
   -content/uploads/2020/10/WP69-Liang_1.pdf

Ma, Yiming, Kairong Xiao, and Yao Zeng. 2022. "Mutual
   Fund Liquidity Transformation and Reverse Flight to
   Liquidity." *Review of Financial Studies.* https://doi.org/10
   .1093/rfs/hhac007

Pan, Kevin, and Yao Zeng. 2019. "ETF Arbitrage under Liquidity Mismatch." Working paper. https://papers.ssrn.com/sol3/
   papers.cfm?abstract_id=2895478

Zeng, Yao. 2017. "A Dynamic Theory of Mutual Fund Runs and
   Liquidity Management." ESRB Working Paper 42, European
   Systemic Risk Board, Frankfurt.

Zhu, Qifei. 2021. "Capital Supply and Corporate Bond
   Issuances: Evidence from Mutual Fund Flows." *Journal of
   Financial Economics* 141 (2): 551–72.

INTERNATIONAL MONETARY FUND

View the latest IMF Publications Catalog to learn more about new titles covering the global economy.

Mention code **Winter22** to receive a **25% discount** for orders placed online at *bookstore.IMF.org*.

IMF PUBLICATIONS
Fall–Winter 2022–23

IMF.org/pubs

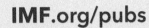

IMF.org/pubs

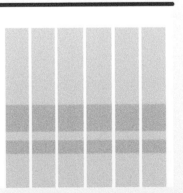